DRIVE
YOUR PEOPLE
WILD
WITHOUT
DRIVING THEM
CRAZY

Other books by Jennifer White

*Work Less, Make More: Stop Working So Hard and
Create the Life You Really Want!*

JENNIFER **WHITE**

DRIVE
YOUR PEOPLE
WILD
WITHOUT
DRIVING THEM
CRAZY

LEADERSHIP LESSONS FOR A CHAOTIC WORLD

CAPSTONE

First published 2001 by
Capstone Publishing Ltd (A John Wiley & Sons Co.)
8 Newtec Place
Magdalen Road
Oxford OX4 1RE
United Kingdom
http://www.capstoneideas.com

British Library Cataloguing in Publication Data
A CIP catalogue record for this book is available from the British Library

ISBN 1-84112-143-6

Typeset by
Forewords, 109 Oxford Road, Cowley, Oxford
Printed and bound by
T.J. International Ltd, Padstow, Cornwall

This book is printed on acid-free paper

Contents

To my clients, both past and present, who are a constant source of inspiration.

To my coaching team, who force me every single day to change, evolve and grow into the leader I can be.

To Steve, the man who has always believed in me.

I am blessed to have you all in my life.

Acknowledgements

There was a time in my life when I thought I was the one responsible for my success. I worked hard. I used my creative ability to come up with hot new ideas. I was the one who woke up in the middle of the night sweating about my business. The one who worried about cash flow, high growth problems and what needed to get done. But the truth is anyone who has had any success at all is surrounded by supportive, amazing people. It is because of these folks that I am who I am today.

FIRST, I WANT TO thank my clients, the people I've personally worked with through the years. Coaching you has taught me how to truly live, how to go for it no matter what the odds, how to stand strong in the middle of chaos and adversity. The impact you've had in my life shows up on every page.

To my RESULTS Development Team – Vickie Bevenour, Darlene Caplan, Abby Donnelly, Chris Fisher, Ken Kesslin,

Terry Kozlowski, Anita Maltbia, JoAnne Myers, Ron Mudge, Pam Ragland, Nan Franks Richardson, Diane Scholten and Nancy Wilkie. This powerful group of coaches brought substance and depth to my work. You endured my typos, constant questions and early morning email with such grace and finesse. Thank you for your substantial contribution to this book.

To my coaching team, those maverick coaches who force me to have courage and strength as we expand into brand new areas. There's nothing like a group of coaches to remind you how much you don't know and how much you still have to learn. That's a gift every CEO needs.

To Celia Rocks at Rocks–DeHart Communications. Celia, you were the one who pushed me to write this book, and boy, you were so right.

To Susan Johnson, my incredible executive assistant. I've searched for a long time for someone like you, and I'm blessed to have you working by my side. I appreciate how you keep things moving along despite the times when I get in the way.

To three women who have been my personal coaches through the years: Madeleine Homan, Shirley Anderson and Nan O'Connor. You showed up in my life at just the right time to teach me how to believe in myself. Thank you for sharing your wisdom and insights with me. To the folks at Coach University and the International Coach Federation, a group of people who introduced coaching to the world.

To Rob Daumeyer, who was the first editor to give me the opportunity to write 700 words a week for my column. I know I gush a lot about you, but you have no idea how giving me the chance to be a columnist opened up my creative spirit. And to every single editor I work with, thank you. You are the bridge to my readers, and I'm appreciative of all your support.

To my editor Mark Allin for your guidance and support in publishing this book. I talked to many publishing folks about this idea, Mark, and you're the only one who truly got my message. To my agent John Willig for sharing your insightful marketing mind with me. I was ready to give up on the publishing world until you stepped in and showed me how to play the game. I am forever grateful for your skills in navigating my writing career.

To my mother who never stopped believing I'd someday be a published author and to my father who gave me my gift of creativity. To Darlene and John White, my in-laws, who support me by coming to booksignings, clipping newspaper articles and enduring my constantly changing career.

To Steve, my husband, who came up with the title for this book. You're the one person in my life who is able to steady me when I'm crazed. You remind me what matters, and you have taught me how to be who I want to be. I love you.

And to you, the reader. I am in awe of your decision to become a leader. You're on a long and winding road, and I'm grateful you chose to spend some of your precious time with me.

Please get in touch and tell me what you think of this book. I wrote it for you.

Introduction

I was sitting in my office going through a stack of paper a few months ago when my phone rang. It was one of my clients. And he was frantic.

SAM STARTED OUR conversation by saying, "Jen, it's awful. You're not going to believe what happened." No hello, no "How are you?" Just frustration and annoyance.

Whenever my clients start a conversation like that, I know I need to sit down, take a deep breath and brace myself for the onslaught. Business has a tendency to push our buttons from time to time, and I knew Sam was having a bad day.

He continued, "They quit. Three of my top salespeople quit!"

Now you don't know Sam, and you don't understand what a disaster this was going to be. Sam is a senior executive with a fast-growing company. His company had plans to go public just six months from the time he called me that day, and the entire executive team was extremely focused on producing results. The more results, the higher the price of their stock. Here Sam was with three of his top-producing sales folks leaving when he was at such a critical juncture. His sales reps hit their breaking point, and they walked.

But here's the real kicker: These three sales reps left close to $1 million on the table. When the company went public six months later, they had the potential to each earn $1 million in stock options. Maybe more.

It seems ludricious, doesn't it? We've all heard the stories of people racing to dot-coms to become instant millionaires. And despite what has happened to those companies, the quest for quick cash kept many people working way too hard 24/7.

Why would these three salespeople leave so much on the table? Ah, such a good question. It's the same one Sam kept asking over and over again. Sam was perplexed (and of course, mad). He screamed, "Are they crazy? They left millions of dollars to have a life?"

The reality is these sales reps weren't willing to sacrifice their lives for the money they could earn when the IPO went through. Is having a fulfilling life more important than money? To these three salespeople, it was.

Now I know that you're finding this story hard to believe. As a leader, you're used to facing the tough times. You're conditioned to push past the pain so you can get the result you want. There are probably even a few of you out there who are thinking the same thing Sam was thinking: Are these people crazy?

In today's economy, these types of things happen all the time. For those of you who brush off this story as just an example of how unreliable salespeople can be, pay attention. One of my clients, Adam, a CEO for a large Fortune 100 company, called me in a bit of a huff a few months ago. It seems the executive he had designated as his successor had decided enough was enough. He was tired of working long hours. He was tired of not being home to see his kids play soccer, cook dinner with his wife and going on vacation without his laptop. He walked into Adam's office and told him he was taking another job so he could get a life.

Yes, the message was Adam had no idea how to create a high-performing organization and still give his people time to enjoy their family and friends. His driving personality drove his No. 1 guy right out the door.

Good thing Adam is smart enough to see a problem when it smacks him on the head. He immediately sped up the process I was coaching him on to harness the power of his people and their performance.

And just the other day I heard a story about a woman who went into her manager's office to ask for flex time. She wanted to put forty hours into a four-day work week in order to spend more time with her kids. She was tired of having to juggle demands at work and home, and she knew having three full days to focus on her family was the right decision.

Now this employee is what we call a top producer. She's the type of woman we'd like to have working for us. In fact, we want an entire team of this type of performer. But her manager didn't know how to deal with her request. He said, "Look, I know you have three children, but I have kids, too. You don't see me working four days a week."

He turned her down. She left two weeks later to become a free agent. She wanted freedom, and her manger didn't know how to give it to her.

The world has changed. Employees know they can leave a job one day and have a better position the next. Gone are the days when you could place an ad in the paper and replace your people in a snap.

Yet here's what I also know: as the leader, you want results. You *need* results. If you don't make your financial numbers quarter after quarter, your investors or shareholders will come down hard on you. Business is about profit after all, and growth is the ultimate focus for most company leaders. Markets are constantly changing, customers are more demanding, and your business model needs work. You barely have time to read your email let alone put together a long-range strategic plan. You don't even have the luxury you once did to hang out until the bad times go away. Your investors think about this quarter's numbers, and they won't wait for a bad cycle to turn around.

It's no wonder you're pushing your people to the limits with the pressure you're under.

Yet at the same time, your employees want a life. They're tired of working eighty-hour work weeks. They have families, outside interests and other things to occupy their time –

especially those GenX employees who insist on playing just as hard as they work. It's not unheard that one of your key employees asks for a six-month sabbatical to travel the world. The old belief that you have to struggle and sacrifice to reach the company's goals doesn't have the appeal it once did.

Add in the fact that you would *personally* like to stop burning the midnight oil and get a life, and you have a real problem on your hands. The world has changed dramatically in the last ten years, and sometimes it seems as if you're not just caught between a rock and a hard place, but that you live there, too. Can you figure out a way to get it all?

I think you can. At my company, The JWC Group Inc., we've spent the last five years developing an executive coaching program to guide you to the results you want. I've seen massive changes happen when leaders step back with our guidance to take a good hard look at how they're showing up. We make our living coaching leaders like you to drive results, keep your talent inspired and get everyone home in time for dinner. What we know is the old techniques of retaining your people and getting results don't work anymore. You've seen this, I'm sure, in your own organization. How you used to lead gives you a big fat nothing today. Why? Because your employees have changed, and most leaders simply don't know how to lead in today's economy.

THE NEW EMPLOYEE

Here's the truth: our employees aren't the same people they used to be. In the past, there was a belief if you worked for a company for thirty years, you'd be able to retire and live comfortably the rest of your life. That idea went out years ago as corporate downsizing spread like wildfire in the late 1980s. The beliefs that employees relied on – loyalty and security – crashed. At the same time, entrepreneurship exploded. People started their own companies. According to the current research, one in twelve people in the United States has started their own businesses. I believe many of these folks were spurred to start their own companies so they could control their lives and not get caught up in having a big organization take care of them.

And then came the Internet. Our society soon became obsessed with the innovative business mavericks who defied all odds and beat the big boys at their own game. People like Jeff Bezos from Amazon and Steve Case at AOL have become household names. Okay, so some of you would argue that the market has taken care of the get-rich-quick stories as stock prices at these companies have struggled since the early gold rush days. Never disregard the influence the dot-com stories have had on your people.

In addition to being influenced by the fast-moving Internet companies, your team lives in a world that now operates 24/7. You no longer have to wait for anything, and you're caught up in getting things done faster, sooner and better. Instant gratification has become the norm, and it impacts every aspect of the organization.

The reality is your employees have been changed by these experiences. They are no longer the "suck it up so someday I'll retire" bunch. They see other people getting flexible work schedules, taking a six-month sabbatical, owning a piece of the company, performing at high levels and being hand-somely rewarded, and they say to themselves, "If that guy can do it, there's no reason I can't, too." And they're right to believe that.

Your employees want flexibility, freedom and ownership. They're willing to ask for what they want – and walk away if they don't come to some agreement. They no longer have a problem saying, "Screw you. I'll work somewhere else." Can you imagine an employee doing that, say 20 years ago?

A maverick spirit has come alive in their souls, and unless you change how you lead, you'll lose that spirit to another job down the street. Frankly, I'm glad those dead spirits have finally arisen. It's a much more exhilarating workplace when people are alive, feisty and involved.

But that leaves the leaders in quite a quandary. You need results, your income depends on the performance of your people, but you're not sure you want to be at their mercy. It's no fun as a leader to work with a bunch of whiney, spoiled employees. Don't think that I'm going to tell you to love your people, and every-thing will be fine. It won't. They need you to lead. They need to create a powerful vision, harness their strengths, inspire their spirits and take them into the market with fire and zest.

That's exactly the problem. You're not doing what they need you to do. It's the leaders in our organizations who are screwing things up, and frankly, you're the problem.

You didn't think I'd hit you right between the eyes so early, did you?

The truth is, as a company leader, you're the problem. You're the one who's driving your people crazy and preventing them from achieving wild success. You're the one who tells your staff you want them to have a life, but you schedule weekend conference calls. You're the one who says you want to inspire them to achieve new heights, but you keep them stuck in the same old jobs. On one hand, you tell them you believe in open book management, but you get livid when they talk about salaries on their lunch breaks. And let's not talk about your challenge with micromanaging, microdoing and just plain lack of trust in their abilities.

But don't just take my word on it. Gallup says that 70 percent of employees quit their manager, not their company. The Hudson Institute says a third of your workers are not planning on staying with you for more than a year. Exit interviews reveal the top two reasons a person quits are: (1) "I wasn't challenged," (2) "My boss was a jerk."

Now I don't want you to put down this book and walk away in a huff thinking that too much rests on your shoulders. I do not believe leaders wake up in the morning with the intention to drive their people crazy. You don't look for ways to slow progress, hinder your people or create long working hours on purpose. Your behavior is unconscious. It's your blind spot. And it's hard as heck to see what you're really doing so you can change how you lead.

I'm a big believer that if there's a problem, there's always a solution. A few years ago, I started promoting my first book, *Work Less, Make More®: Stop Working So Hard and Create the Life You Really Want!* It's a book that helps you have the time and money to make more of your life. At the time I wrote the book, I was personally coaching individuals how to break their obsession with work. I worked in the trenches every day helping my clients create amazing careers while building fulfilling lives. I had hundreds of success stories from my years of coaching, and I decided to write it all down in a book.

Something interesting happened along the way. Every single time I spoke about Work Less, Make More® or coached a manager or leader to achieve this goal, they always said, "Hey, can you teach my employees to do the same thing?" Sometimes they'd say: "What would it take to bring this program into my company?" But that question was soon followed by, "Can we call it something besides Work Less, Make More®? I'm not sure that's the message I want to send to my team."

They had this illusion that I was going to teach their staff how to sit back and eat bon-bons all day long.

I did the next best thing. I started experimenting with my clients to figure out a way to bring the Work Less, Make More® philosophy into their organizations. I became obsessed with the answers to these questions: What's the real reason people feel the need to give up their lives for their work? What's the underlying problem every company faces in trying to create results and still make it home in time for dinner? How can we create an organization that gives us everything we want: results, talented people and time for a life?

As my coaching team and I did more and more work with organizations, I discovered the old adage that fish begin to stink at the top is true. Employees have changed, yet most of the leaders we worked with were using leadership techniques developed fifty years ago. I uncovered what stops progress, the stuff we all do that prevents our employees from being amazing. And I started to see all the things I personally do to stifle my own company's success.

Here's a quick assessment you can take to find out if you're driving your people wild or if you're driving them crazy. You just may find a few things you can work on to create a high-performing team without dealing with high turnover and burned out employees.

THE WILD OR CRAZY QUIZ

I'm not foolish enough to think this is the first leadership book you've ever read, and I know some of you have been at this game for a long, long time. This book will work if you're a brand new leader or an old-timer. Just take a few minutes to determine how you're doing right now with the skills you'll need to drive results, keep your people and still have time for everyone to have a life.

As you go through the quiz below, put a checkmark next to each item that applies to you. *Check everything that applies. And please, be a hard grader.* It won't do you any good if you aren't willing to accurately assess where you are right now.

You'll notice a number next to each of the statements on this quiz. That refers to a corresponding chapter that will help you overcome your problem areas. If you see a lot of checkmarks with (3) after them, for example, flip to Chapter 3 first.

☐ You'll often hear me say: "This is the world of the Internet. We don't have time to wait." (1)

☐ Chaos rules our organization. We all feel as if we're running around with too much to do. (1)

☐ My people fight their own battles. I'm here to guide them, not defend them. (1)

☐ My department is understaffed, but I haven't reduced the workload or the goals. We'll have to keep our nose to the grindstone to get done what we need to get done. (1)

☐ I sometimes secretly wish I was a dictator, and my team would just follow my orders. (1)

☐ I know more than anyone else in my department. Let's keep it that way. (1)

☐ I like knowing I can save the day no matter what happens. I often do. (1)

☐ I tend to change my mind a lot. Things are constantly changing, and my decisions need to change with them. (2)

☐ People have told me I'm inconsistent, that they can't predict how I'm going to react to situations. I think that keeps them alert and on their toes. (2)

☐ I often call my staff on nights and weekends. (2)

☐ I schedule conference calls with my team before 7 am, after 6 pm and sometimes on weekends. (2)

☐ My cell phone is with me at all times – and I answer it no matter what the time of day. (2)

☐ I pretend to care about how my employee are, but I really don't. We have too much work to do than spend time socializing. (2)

☐ When something needs to get done and my team isn't doing it right, I often jump in and handle the situation. (2)

☐ I can't tell you what inspires each member of my team to perform at the highest level. We have work to do. There's no time for these touchy-feely exercises. (2)

☑ I'm a firm believer if only my staff would learn how to better manage their time, they would get a lot more done. (3)

☑ I can't remember the last time I worked a 40-hour work week. (3)

☐ My people can't either. (3)

☐ My team spends 80 percent of their time in meetings. (3)

☐ I rarely work from home. I need to be in the office to handle crises. (3)

☐ You'd never find me siting down with my staff every week (or every two weeks) to review what they're working on and how to prioritize what's most important. There's no time for that. (3)

☐ I have an open door policy so I never shut my door. People are coming in and out of my office all day long. (3)

☑ We work at a very intense pace in my company, and it's rare we give ourselves time to rest. (4)

☑ Everything is a priority. And most of it has to be done right now. (4)

☑ Many times I feel like a firefighter. I tend to rush around putting out fires all day long. (4)

☐ My people don't really have the resources they need to get the job done. We're lean and mean around here. (4)

☑ I'd love to slow things down, but our investors, shareholders and/or CEO won't allow it. (4)

☐ I don't know what every person on my team is gifted at in their work. Getting results, that's what matters. (5)

☑ I'm good at a lot of things, but not a master at anything. (5)

☐ I sometimes wonder why I'm doing this job. Why aren't I more jazzed by more work? (5)

☐ My people seem to have a balanced set of skills. I don't understand why we're not producing better results. (5)

☐ I hold back information and only communicate on a need-to-know basis. (6)

☐ I communicate with my team primarily by email. It's rare we meet face- to-face. (6)

☑ If you ask anyone on my team, they will probably give you a different answer on where we're headed. (6)

☐ I get frustrated when I tell my people something once or twice, and they don't do anything about it. Why can't they become better listeners? (6)

☐ It's been more than one year since I've been on vacation for longer than a week. (7)

☑ I often take my laptop home with me. (7)

☑ My family tells me I work too much. The problem is I don't see how I can reduce my hours when there's so much to do. (7)

☑ Home in time for dinner? Yeah, right. (7)

There are times I feel exhausted and tired of it all. And I know my people feel the same way. (7)

NOW WHAT?

When you were taking this quiz, I bet some stuff started to pop up for you. That's what we call clarity, and it's a good thing.

We both know there are times when you want to blame your team for their mistakes or for weak performance. You want to believe that if they would just learn better time-management skills, they wouldn't have to work so many hours. You convince yourself that if only you and your team could make that huge performance goal, blow past company expectations, then you could all scale back and get some breathing room. (It never happens, does it?)

You have probably created a whole bunch of reasons why you're not getting the results you want. Or why you're getting the results you want and how it's worth the price you're paying. You've probably even told yourself that when key talent leaves, it's not your fault but a bigger and better opportunity really is out there for them. You even convince yourself they'll be better off in another place.

Give me a break. The world has changed, and every day I see leaders who are trying to lead the same ol' way. It's not working anymore, is it? If you really want to drive results, keep your key talent and give everyone time for a life, you need to take a good hard look in the mirror. Yes, at yourself.

This book – and our executive coaching program – is the

answer to the question: "So if I'm the problem, now what do I do?"

YOUR QUIZ RESULTS

Now go back to the Leadership Quiz on page 10 and re-read the questions. Take a close look at the items you checked. What are the top three main things that hold you back from being an inspiring leader? Write them down here.

1.

2.

3.

The best way to use this book is to look at the three things that are big thorns in your side and take care of them first. It's often better to go after the behaviors that cause the most problems. You'll feel the biggest relief when you handle these issues first.

WHAT'S NEXT

I've outlined our innovative seven-step process to help you not only change how you lead in today's economy, but give you the results you want. Yes, I'm going to ask you to change how you operate. You'll need to take a good hard look at how you're managing so you can stop getting in the way of your team's performance. You will have to stop micromanaging, being a control freak and jumping in to save the day. I will ask you to change what you believe about leadership, success and what truly matters.

And you thought this book was going to be all about how to motivate your employees! It's about changing how *you* lead. It's about helping you identify the mistakes you're making so you can move into a new way of operating. And it's about taking on a new way of operating so you can get the outcomes you want despite the changes you're dealing with on a daily basis.

Please understand I'm not standing here to tell you I have been the ideal leader. There have been times in my business when *I'm* the world's most atrocious leader. I've made just about every mistake possible – like not training my staff then getting mad that they make a mistake, having way too many priorities that are all perceived as urgent, overreacting to stupid problems, being inaccessible or not paying attention when my staff is talking to me, blowing off their requests, taking forever to make decisions. I've also done some great things as a leader, really inspiring things. Like you, I'm still making mistakes and tweaking how I lead. That's part of growing as a leader: learning how to continually expand and grow.

When I started developing this program, the first place I applied it was my own life. You'll never find me giving advice I haven't tried or used myself. A huge part of leadership is walking the talk, and I hold myself to that same standard. But sometimes I wish we would wake up one day, and all of a sudden be the perfect leader. Unfortunately, it doesn't work that way. Being a powerful leader takes work. You'll make gut-wrenching decisions, and you'll have to make the tough calls. And you'll definitely have to admit that you were wrong. A lot.

My point of asking you to take a good hard look in the mirror is not to drag you down. This is not an excuse to beat yourself up more than you do already. What I'm attempting to do is wake you up to identify where you can improve your own skills so you build healthier, saner work environments.

This is not an easy program, but if you're serious about driving results in your company – and retaining your employees – then we both know you'll do what it takes.

Sam took my advice and got amazing results, but you'll learn more about him later. Just know, with the same effort, you too can *Drive Your People Wild Without Driving Them Crazy*™.

YOUR 90-DAY FOCUS

One of the best ways to use this book is to have a goal, a target, you want to reach with your team. It's one thing to read a good book and pass it around to your friends. It's quite another to apply the concepts so you see a difference in your work – and in your life. Maybe it's the coach in me coming out, but I want you to use this book. These concepts won't mean anything unless you put them into action right away. The best way to do that is to define what results you want to achieve.

Take a few minutes and decide what you most want to accomplish as a leader during the next 90 days. No, I'm not going to ask you to give me your entire business plan or even your yearly targets. Let's use a short timeframe, 90 days, to see if this *Drive Your People Wild Without Driving Them Crazy*™ philosophy works for you as it has with so many other leaders.

What result do you most want to reach with your team in the next three months? It could be improving customer satisfaction levels or transitioning easily through a new organizational structure that's coming down the pike. Perhaps you want to exceed your quarterly numbers or put your team through an extensive business planning process without the typical "we're too busy to do that" comments. Maybe it's as easy as enjoying the process of giving performance evaluations, something you truly dread.

Make sure this target is something that impacts the bottom line and truly matters to you. You'll be using the ideas in this book as a way to accomplish this goal more easily than you did before.

Take out a pen and write in your goal:

During the next 90 days, we will achieve . . .

A strategy for producing results in a timely fashion through an organized process balancing structure & creative freedom

The secret to setting this target is to make sure it's measurable. How will you know you've reached success? If you can answer that question, you have the right goal. If not, go back and try it again.

DO YOU WANT TO BE A LEADER?

Before we jump into the strategies to drive results and keep your people happy, I have a question to ask: are sure you want to be the leader?

Many times I see folks promoted into positions of authority because they were performers. What happens is these performers liked being the superstar, but the natural progression in their companies was to "climb the corporate ladder."

Let me give you an example. One of my clients, Robert, was the director of e-commerce for a Fortune 500 company. Robert is the type of guy who is amazing at what he does. He talks fast, walks fast and thinks fast. (My type of guy!) He's on the cutting edge, always on the lookout for new ways of operating. He devours leading magazines like *Fast Company* and *Wired*, and he knows just about everything you'd ever want to know about the Internet and e-commerce. He once told me he was the only guy at his company who truly got what e-commerce is about. Pretty scary if you're the CEO of a major Fortune 50 company, and you only have one guy who gets the ever-changing marketplace. (But that's another story.)

The main problem with Robert was not that he didn't produce results. He does. All the time. The problem was Robert was a poor manager. No, not because he couldn't learn how to be a good leader. Robert is so talented, he could learn to be a master at anything. The fundamental truth was Robert didn't want to lead. He thrives in environments where he can show up and share his brilliant mind with the people around him. Like most of us, he was naturally drawn to the areas where he could use his brilliance.

So here's what happened: Robert was so busy being the e-commerce expert at his company that he was constantly on the road. In Asia one week, San Jose the next and then squeezing in a day trip to Boston. His staff never had enough time with him to learn how they could support the company's e-commerce movement. Most of them were floundering around trying to find their way. When they were in meetings with Robert, he naturally jumped into the superstar role and took over. You can imagine how valued his team felt. On one hand, they were in awe of Robert's ability to answer any question and shape such a compelling vision. On the other hand, they were frustrated because they were never given the chance to shine.

Did they tell him? Sure, and Robert really did want to change. But he was too busy being the performer. He was on a plane doing the job his team should have been doing. He didn't think he could take the time to teach his people how to duplicate his success.

This chaotic cycle never stopped because Robert didn't take the time to work with his staff. He didn't train his team how to expand the company's e-commerce vision, and Robert was forced to manage by email and voicemail rather than having intimate conversations. He spent too much time being the expert and not enough time managing his team. No wonder he was overworked, exhausted and running around in circles.

When I asked Robert why he was a manager, he said, "Jen, this is the only way I can move up in the organization. I need to lead a team in order to get authority and responsibility. This is just part of the career path at this company."

Yuk. There's nothing worse than working for a manager who's

only doing it to further a career. After two years of work with me, Robert finally admitted to himself – and to me – that he didn't want to be a manager. Not that he couldn't learn how to be a great manager, but he just didn't *want* to. So he left his secure corporate job to become a consultant and leverage his strengths as a superstar. I've never seen him happier in his life.

I know, you were hoping I would tell you a story about a terrible manager who evolved into being a powerful leader. I'll tell you some of those stories later in this book. My point in sharing Robert's story is to get you to see that not everyone is cut out to be a good manager. Robert is a leader of darn good ideas. He's not a leader of people. And that's a very important distinction.

If you want to *Drive Your People Wild Without Driving Them Crazy*™, then you must learn how to be an inspiring leader of people. First you need to decide if you want it bad enough. Do you want to do what it takes to be an inspiring leader? Why? Before you continue reading, I want you to stop reading and answer this question: Why do you want to become an inspiring leader? What's the real reason?

Even if it takes you two years to come up with an answer, do not continue reading this book until you've answered that question. Unless you know why you're doing something, you will not have the capacity to make the changes you need to make.

This seven-point process is brutal. It's hard, hard work. And unless you have a compelling reason why you're going to change just about everything you do in order to get better results while having happy employees, you will not succeed.

So I ask again: Why do you want to become an inspiring leader? When, you're ready write down your answer here:

I am willing to do what it takes to be an inspiring leader because . . .

ONE FINAL NOTE

Don't be afraid to use this book. Don't be afraid to scribble on the pages. Don't be afraid to cross things out. Change your mind. Explore new areas. Make a mess of these pages. Write ideas all over the place. That's what you're supposed to do. Redesigning how you lead is a messy and chaotic process. It won't do you any good to read all the pages here if you're not willing to take action. Applying these concepts to your life takes action. Are you willing to do what it takes to get the results you want?

Ah, I thought your answer would be yes.

Put on your seatbelts. We have lots of work to do.

CHAPTER 1

Transform chaos into sanity

We live in a stressful and confusing time. In most organizations, large and small, chaos rules. Business models change overnight. We launch new products in less than 30 days, completely overhaul our computer systems in a week and spin off new profit centers with an idea and a prayer. Competitors sprout up every day to attack our customer base, Internet start-ups keep trying to shift distribution systems, and our customers change their minds overnight. If we work in small companies, chaos definitely triumphs because we never have enough resources to do it the "right" way, so we do it with what we've got.

EVEN THE PEOPLE around us are continually changing. Right when you think you know whom to call to deal with a problem, you discover that person is no longer with the company. Or they've taken a new role that has nothing to do with what you need right then.

This never-ending chaos creates insanity. It's no wonder people are walking around with a dazed look in their eyes. The next time you're in a staff meeting, take a moment to really look at your people. They're working too much. They're stressed out and burned out, and they've been this way for a while. I don't know about you, but I see a real problem brewing unless you as the leader find a way to create some sanity amidst the chaos.

Yet the truth is that chaos is crucial for creativity to thrive. If there's one thing success in today's economy is all about, it's that: hot new ideas. To compete in the marketplace, you must have a new approach, a way to rise above the noise so your customers pay attention to your product offerings. It's vital that you have some chaos, disorder and flexibility to give your people free rein to develop the next million dollar idea. We know that too much structure and too many rules crush the creative spirit.

On the other side of the fence, businesses thrive with consistency. You need to have a strong infrastructure to support company growth. Once you promise something to a customer, you better deliver on it or you'll end up like the soon out-of-business dot-com with real problems because efficient processes aren't in place. Customers are waiting way too long for orders. Products are shipped to the wrong people. Companies are losing millions bringing people to their web sites without having the systems in place to fulfill orders or turn those eyeballs into dollars. Their employees start to leave in droves because they see the company isn't going to make it.

This same thing happened in the cellular industry. I used to work for a large cellular company during the early growth stages, and I saw this phenomena unfold first hand. Companies like AT&T, PacTel and Sprint participated in auctions through the FCC and paid millions of dollars – billions of dollars – to earn the right to provide cellular service in various markets. Talk about pressure to get a return on investment! These companies started selling cellular services long before the infrastructure and technology was there to support their products. Soon you were driving down the road negotiating a huge deal on your cell phone when boom! Your phone went dead. You were annoyed, frustrated, and you've probably even spoke a few choice words to express your anger. Yet the exact same thing happened when digital cellular service showed up. The pressure to get solid returns on such a huge capital investment forced companies to go live with their service before the technology could fully support their users.

Does that mean that you throttle down and wait until the processes and systems are built before you take the company to the next level? Of course not. Today's economy is not about sleep walking. It's about running. There are too many gurus out there telling you to slow down, take it easy and let nature take its course. The world of the Internet doesn't allow that if you want to be the best of the best.

The answer is to create sanity in a chaotic world without destroying the creative, flexible culture your people need. That's what we're all seeking as leaders: how to walk the fine line between chaos, creativity and sanity. As a leader, it's your job to figure out a way to win again and again in a permanently disruptive world. The secret is to balance these two seemingly contradictory forces to create a sane and results-focused work environment. To do that, you need to *transform* your leadership style.

TRANSFORMATION? WHAT DOES THAT MEAN?

When I use the word transformation, I'm referring to a radical shift. This isn't a natural transition from a chaotic environment to one with structure and order. When you transition from one thing to another, you're moving to the next level or evolving to a new stage. Most people today think of change as getting bigger or better. They see themselves transitioning from being the staffer to supervisor to manager to director to vice-president to CEO, taking on bigger and better roles with each step. When looking at their crazed work environment, some leaders believe the old adage, "This too shall pass." That's called a transition. You believe that today we're chaotic, tomorrow things will settle down and all will be well.

Wrong! Business is moving at such a frenzied pace that we don't naturally transition into a more calm environment anymore. In the past, this philosophy was true. Today it's not because business is moving too darn fast to allow natural transitions to occur.

Transforming how you lead means you're changing fundamental pieces of how you operate in order to alter the nature of how the job is done. You're trashing the old and creating a new set of rules. Chaos becomes transformation in action.

Let me move out of this philosophical la-la land and give you some real ideas to chew on. I was speaking to a group of CEOs one afternoon when a very important question popped up. Someone asked, "How do I lead when I'm a dinosaur?" Many leaders in today's economy are dealing with people who know a lot more than they do about the job at hand. Things change so fast, there's no way a leader can stay on top of these advances. They'll die trying if they try at all.

In the past, leaders used to move up the corporate ladder in a natural transition. They would do one job, get really good at it and then move into other positions until finally they arrived into management. Their careers were built by moving to the next level on the organizational chart based on the expertise they picked up along the way. People who got promoted quickly were able to assimilate new skills in record time, and they became masters at knowing what to do.

One of my clients, Greg, had a real issue with this when we first started working together. Greg is the vice-president of sales for a traditional manufacturing firm, and when he first showed up, he was stressed. His human resources manager, also a client of ours, took him out to lunch and told him he had to get a grip or his health was in jeopardy. He started working with me a few days later to maintain results and get a life.

As we began working together, it became quite clear that Greg was struggling with this "I have to know the answer to every question" belief. He thought that when the general manager or president of the company asked him a question, he needed to know the answer. In minute detail. Consequently, Greg spent hours reading memos and email to get himself up-to-speed on what was going on. The reality? He didn't have enough time to know everything. He was stressing himself out trying to know the answers.

In the past, this was what leaders did. Not anymore. Today you only know bits and pieces of what their people know. It's not your job to be experts anymore, it's your job to lead their people and harness their collective brainpower. But you haven't transformed how you lead, and you're stuck in a time warp.

Today Greg spends his time focused on planning and executing strategy and forging the path for the company's future. No more silly details for him. That's what his people are for.

Instead of admitting that you need to change their leadership style, you bring craziness to the organization. You take too long to make decisions. You make your people pull together pages of PowerPoint slides to explain every little thing that's going on. You jump in to do the work you hired them to do because you feel more comfortable doing than leading. You get in the way, have no idea where the company is going and make your people start and stop projects all day long. Forget about focus, you're too busy trying to justify you position as the boss. And you're driving their people crazy in the process.

The truth is you feel inadequate because you're no longer the expert. You closed your eyes for just a minute, and the world went flying by. Rather than admit your fear that your people are more brilliant than you, you cover it all up by micromanaging, microdoing and creating barriers. Deep inside, you believe if you get enough information, read enough books or go to enough technology conferences, you'll finally understand the nuances of your people's work.

You know what I'm going to say about that: fat chance.

Leaders are the ones creating the chaos. Why? Because you think that's how you're supposed to transition in our technologically advanced society. Do you see the vicious cycle that shows up in your organization? What you don't get is this isn't about transitioning to a new place. Leadership today demands a new approach. It's time to transform how you lead.

WHAT YOU'RE DOING THAT CREATES THE CHAOS

Before I share with you how to transform how you lead, you need to take a good look at what you're doing to add to the craziness. I think it's too easy to sit back and believe there's nothing you can do about the constant chaos. "You spent the last few pages outlining all the massive changes impacting my business every day, Jen," you're saying to yourself. "What can I do to influence the entire market?"

Ah, what an easy excuse that is. Blame it on market conditions, the government, fierce competition, whatever. Those are just excuses. As a leader, there is so much you can do, so much that's in your control, to balance chaos and sanity. Wouldn't it be great to produce the results without everyone paying such a high price?

I see leaders every day adding more fuel to an already stressful situation, and it goes from exciting to toxic. That's what we have to stop. Right away. And the first place to look is at your own behavior. What are you doing to add to the already chaotic environment?

Here are some of the common things I see leaders do every day. Do these reflect how you lead?

1. You're an extremely flexible leader who thrives on new ideas. And you're okay with saying, "We'll figure it out later on."

Let me share with you a story about one of my clients. Christine is a fast-moving executive who's at the top of her game. As the COO for an insurance company, Christine is responsible for a 250-person department that's under constant pressure to perform. She often tells me her job feels like she's herding cats.

When I walked into Christine's office for the first time, I immediately knew what her biggest problem was. She was much too flexible. One of the things we often do is spend the day shadowing our clients around the office. That helps us get a real look at how they interact with their teams and how they show up as leaders. As an executive coach, I've developed this ability to sniff out what's truly going on. With Christine, it was clear that she took the idea of being flexible and exaggerated it.

Many times when one of her managers showed up with a new idea, Christine would immediately put on her creativity hat, and she and her manager would further expand the idea. She'd always end the meeting by saying, "Great idea, go for it." Her manager would rush off to try something new with his or her team. Christine didn't ask them to write out a strategic plan or even an action plan. She trusted that they would know how to handle any problems that showed up. As a result, Christine's entire department was constantly starting new projects and never completing programs they had started weeks earlier. Every idea was a good idea in her world.

What Christine failed to do was provide a clear direction for her team. Without that, her 12 managers had their own ideas. Every one of the 250 people were running around doing work that wasn't related or wasn't impactful because the environment was too flexible. They ended up being frustrated and confused, not to mention overloaded with the sheer volume of work the new ideas generated. And yes, chaos ruled the day.

When I first pointed out this challenge to her, Christine was hesitant to establish too many expectations. She wanted to be seen as a leader who listened to her people. She was proud of her team's ability to start many new projects, and she sometimes enjoyed the flexible work environment she had created. She actually told me the chaos was good even if that meant they needed 60-hour work weeks to get everything done. You got it – she was willing to sacrifice her people's lives so chaos could thrive. Not a good thing to do as a leader focused on driving your people wild without driving them crazy.

Yet at the same time, Christine told me she was getting tired of herding the cats. "Everyone has their own opinion," she said, "and it's getting a bit old. What would happen if we were all on the same page?"

There we go! Too much flexibility actually adds too much chaos. There's a fine line between flexibility and order, and Christine needed a lot more structure so her people could focus. That's exactly what we did, and the results of the department soared.

2. Your team is under pressure to produce a certain result, so you jump in at the last minute to add your insights.

No. Don't do it!

Every time I see this happening, that's exactly what I want to yell out loud. Have you ever noticed that once you jump in, everyone has this look of horror on their faces? I promise you, your team is sitting by the coffee machine or on the email server talking about how you show up at the final hour to muck things up. You're adding chaos to an already complicated process when you let your need to control persuade you to put your nose in where it doesn't belong.

If you can add value that will finalize the project, then by all means, provide input. But make darn sure that you're not adding more hassle to their workload. You'd be surprised how much chaos you bring to a situation when stress levels are high already.

It drives them crazy when you show up at the final hour to get in their way.

3. You believe information is power. So you hold on to it.

You've probably had this happen to you at some point, and I'm sure it got under your skin. This belief that information is power is an old one from the old economy. Yes, information is important. Real power comes from applying that information to get results. Did you get that? Action on the information is what creates the right outcomes in your company.

> **My question: How can your people get the right outcomes without having the necessary information?**

One of the companies we work with is on the fast track. They all seem to be these days, don't they? This small company is run by five bullheaded leaders. The four men and one woman have strong personalities, and they aren't afraid to express their opinions. I must say, that's one of the reasons I personally work with them: their spunk and intensity makes them quite an interesting group.

There's one issue these five leaders deal with every day. You'd think they have challenges with each other as they individually want to be the lead of the pack. In some interesting way, they respect each other so much, that power game doesn't show up among the executive team. But boy, does it ever with their employee base.

These five leaders used to spend hours trying to decide what to share and what not to share with the team. They were afraid to share financial data because they believed their people would gasp at how much money the company was earning. They were afraid to share bad news because they thought morale would take a nose dive. They were afraid to let light shine past the boardroom doors.

These five leaders were so caught up in trying to protect themselves that they didn't give their people the details they needed. They hoarded information under the belief that if they shared too much, their people would use it against them.

You can imagine what their results looked like. They hit a plateau in total revenues and some business units started to lose money for the first time. Worse, their people were walking around in the dark and were not able to make crucial decisions. Instead, issues were brought back to the executive committee and of course, it took weeks to get a decision made. By that time, their people had to run around and get things done at the last minute. Yes, more chaos caused by a slow decision-making process.

What I discovered when I started working with this executive team was their employees didn't understand how their jobs impacted the bottom line, so they put their attention in other places. And the bottom line suffered. Freeing up the information flow created a massive turnaround with that company in less than 12 months.

Let me be clear before we move on: I personally do not believe today's leaders withhold information as a power trip. They don't communicate properly because they're overworked, overloaded and overburdened with everything else on their plates. If communication is a major issue for you, please jump ahead to Chapter 6: Communicate with Power. You're causing more chaos by not effectively communicating.

4. You react to problems rather than responding to them.

This point is especially for the firefighters out there. Do you spend your entire day handling one crisis after another? Rushing from here to there, band aiding this problem and negotiating on another all the while feeling as if you haven't gotten much done? Are you spending the day reacting to what shows up and feeling exhausted by the intensity of it?

Here's what you have to know: reacting is not deciding. When you react to situations, you go into your library of old habits to unconsciously make a choice about what to do. Reactions are usually the first thing that come out of your mouth. You don't think about what you're saying, you just say it. More times than not, reactions cause more problems.

Think of the last time you had a knee-jerk reaction to a prob-lem. One of your staff members came into your office with a major challenge, and you threw out the first thing that came into your head. Your employee rushed out the door to solve the issue, and five other things popped up as the effect of that decision. You thought you were solving a problem; instead, you were creating new ones. That's no way to reduce chaos or the workload in your organization.

As a company leader, how you react to situations has a ripple effect on anyone involved in cleaning up the mess. When someone comes into your office to deliver bad news, do you shoot the messenger? If you do, you're taking your anger about the problem out on the people around you. Which is a reaction, not a response to the problem. Intellectually, you understand it's not their fault. Emotionally, you rant, rave and react rather than admit you're disappointed with the news.

Another way to know if you react to situations is to notice how many times you make a decision then change your mind. In the moment, you say one thing and then later, you say something else. That's reacting – and it drives your people crazy. Stand in their shoes for a moment. You get direction to do one thing then before you know it, your manager has you running off in another direction. Then another one and another one. It's exhausting to keep starting and stopping. Those constant reactions create tremendous chaos in an already overstimulated environment.

Responding is about paying attention. When you react, you focus on one solution which often causes havoc in areas you didn't consider. When you respond, you focus on multiple options and select the one that's right. Responding is what separates the good leaders from the bad.

I'm sure you're thinking that if you had the time, you would respond to more situations. We coach our leaders how to respond to a problem in less than five minutes. If you do it right, it can take you about three minutes to develop three options to choose from and two minutes to decide which path is the right one to take.

THE CHAOTIC LEADER CHECKLIST

There are plenty of other ways that you're adding to the chaos of your organization. Do any of these statements sound like you?

- ☐ You change your mind on a daily basis. The market is changing too fast to stay focused on one path.
- ☐ There are too many priorities and not enough people to get them all done.
- ☐ You call unscheduled meetings on a regular basis.
- ☐ You pull people from assignments and projects and leave the rest of the team to pick up the slack.
- ☐ You try so hard to please the customer, but you don't think about the long-term effect that decision has on the company or your people.
- ☐ You sometimes deliberately create a stressful situation because you secretly believe your people will work harder.
- ☐ You often put off making tough decisions in the hope the situation will resolve itself.
- ☐ You think information is power, and you hold important details back. You need all the power you can get.

☐ You give responsibility to your people, but no authority to make decisions. You're the leader. That's your job.

☐ You don't really trust your people can get the job done, so you jump in to do their work. Not all the time, but when it comes to important situations, of course.

☐ You're too busy to plan. You know that's the right thing to do, but you never seem to find the time.

☐ You're afraid to fail, so you make sure you and the team doesn't.

☐ You spend a ridiculous amount of time trying to stomp out the chaos.

☐ You have no idea what your people think about the current chaos level. Who has time to talk about that?

☐ Your people have told you that you need to delegate more to them. You're resisting.

☐ You thrive on new ideas. And you try to get as many underway as possible.

If these statements sound like you, what an opportunity you have to transform chaos into sanity. It seems you need some more sanity in your life.

YOUR REAL RESPONSIBILITY AS A LEADER

In the past, it was a leader's job to provide training, system, motivation and strategy for their people. You were the expert, the one who knew all the answers, the person in charge. In today's economy, this doesn't exist much any more. What's the real value you're providing to your people? That's the question many of my clients are asking themselves these days. If you're creating a team of people who are much faster, smarter and more knowledgeable than you, what's the value you as the leader contribute? Unless you know the answer to this question, you will not succeed.

Remember, this is about transforming chaos into sanity. You need chaos for creativity to thrive, and your people need sanity so they fall in love with their work again. That's really what they want. They want to love their work – and their lives. And you can help them do that.

Here's what I believe are your six responsibilities are as a leader today. Take these on, and you'll transform how you lead.

1. Be the obstacle remover.

Your No. 1 responsibility from this day forward is to remove obstacles that stand in your people's way. This strategy is the only way you're going to thrive when intellectual capital rules.

Does this sound like someone you know? Perhaps you?

It's a Tuesday morning, and you're reading email when one of your key staff knocks on your door, pops his head in and says, "Do you have a minute?"

He sits down and proceeds to give you a play-by-play analysis of a major problem he's having with another department. It seems the staff there aren't taking his requests as a top priority, and everything he needs from them takes weeks to get done. Your employee is frustrated and annoyed to say the least.

Things have gotten so bad that now your employee is trying to bypass that department to get the data he needs, and he has upset the department's director.

You have two choices at this point. You either (1) coach your employee how to handle the situation or (2) remove the obstacle. Ah, an interesting choice, isn't it? If you coach the employee to sit down with the department head and get embroiled in a dispute, you'll immediately take him off focus on what truly matters. You know there's a much bigger issue going on here than simply not getting the information your team needs, but there's a part of you that says your employee has to learn how to fight his own battles and get the job done.

The other choice is to handle the issue yourself. If you choose to remove the obstacle for this employee, you will have to pile more work onto your already full plate. You also have issues with this same department head, and you're not sure you want to take on the assignment of having to solve this problem. Choice #1 is clearly the better choice for you.

Most leaders would let their people fight their own battles. That is until some huge episode or fight breaks out that forces them to get involved. Don't let this be you. You need to step in and solve the problem – not band-aid the issue – so it stops being an issue.

In the past, you had the luxury of time to allow your people to solve their own problems. That's not the case anymore. If you want to accomplish results in a short period of time – what today's economy demands – you have to stand strong and help your people get the job done.

Think of yourself as RotoRooter. Your employees are working in a long tube trying to get the job done, and you're there to flush out everything that clogs up the flow. If you don't, you're not adding real value. It's your team's responsibility to do their jobs brilliantly. It's your job to create an environment that allows them to shine. You must do anything and everything you can to allow them do their jobs.

The second you let your people get involved in removing obstacles, you frustrate them and take them off focus. Not only will your people feel unsupported, which may force them out the door, but they won't produce the results you both desperately want. You lose on both ends.

You need to transform your leadership style to be the remover of obstacles. It drives them wild when you get rid of everything that prevents them from getting the job done.

Here's a model we use with our clients that works extremely well. It's a five-step process that allows you to work with your team, produce amazing results and drive them wild in the process (Figure 1.1).

Goals

One of the key roles you fulfill with your team is helping them identify what exactly they're doing. What is the goal their job relates to? What's the end point you're trying to reach? Your

Figure 1.1 Smash through those obstacles

people need to be clear on what they're trying to accomplish. They can figure out how to get there, but first they need to know what they're aiming for.

Obstacles

A great exercise before you start taking action is to identify the things that could possibly get in the way of producing results. Most people wait until the fire is raging before they do anything. That's not the way to lead in today's world. Be a proactive leader to draw out obstacles that could get in the way and find solutions before problems arise.

Action Plan

Once you have the goal in place, you can easily work with your team to strategize what actions they need to take to get the job done. These action plans will change every day based on market conditions, but this exercise allows your team to get clear on what needs to get done.

Move

Yes, the world according to Nike: Just do it.

Tweak

This is where you as the leader show up to help develop new strategies, identify new obstacles, change direction, whatever. You're tweaking the system as you go along, and you can play a high-level role in this process.

The reality is your team does the work. You as the leader need to spend the majority of your time on eliminating obstacles that get in their way and prevent them from being brilliant. Just as you're rewarded in the marketplace with your customers for giving them what they want quicker and easier than anyone else, you need to apply this same concept to your people.

No one takes the time to remove the obstacles, and it's the real value you can contribute to your team. In an overly complex world, the leader's role is to simplify, reduce tension and allow brilliance to shine through, Your people don't have the leverage or the time to focus on this, but you sure can.

Action step

Use the Smash Through Those Obstacles model I introduced as a way to shift your behavior from problem delegator to obstacle remover. In your next staff meeting, walk your team through the five-step process and help them identify what obstacles are getting in their way – or what possible blocks they see. What a great thing for you to focus on: stopping the obstacles before they arrive. You may be surprised at what your people perceive to be obstacles. And you'll immediately increase your stock in their eyes by handling issues before they become problems.

2. Give your people a single laser focus.

Your people aren't just overworked. They're overstimulated.

If you think you're dealing with issues of too much chaos, multiply that by 100 and you get an idea of what your people are experiencing. Every day they show up to hundreds of email, memos, faxes and pages. They open business magazines only to discover there's some new technology that could dramatically impact their work, and they're off learning the details about it. They are bombarded with new technogadets, assignments to take on, software to learn, meetings to attend, committees to serve on and ideas bouncing around in their heads that they want to try. And don't forget all the times you walk into their offices saying, "Boy, do I have a great project for you." Overstimulated hardly covers it.

The reason chaos spirals out of control is your people are rushing off in too many directions, trying to get way too much done in a 10-hour day. What are you doing to keep them on focus?

Ah, that's what I thought. Not much.

The real value you can bring to your team in this new world is this: Focus. Transform your leadership style from being the one dolling out assignments to the one identifying opportunities. As the leader, you're in a unique position to know exactly what's going on in the company. You interface with different business units, and you understand the entire scope of what the company is trying to accomplish.

How many times have you told your people to complete a project only to kill it when it was almost complete? You get my point.

Your people need you to direct the course of their work. I didn't say do their work, I said provide strategic, high-level and much-needed direction on where they need to spend their time. Give them a single laser focus and help them stay the course. Chaos immediately turns into sanity because they know what they're doing and how it impacts company results.

Action step

If focus is a real issue for you and your team, it's time to jump ahead to Chapter 3: Maximize Productivity. You'll find a great method to use to focus your attention – and your team – on the activities that matter. This is a necessary skill for any leader to learn who constantly deals with ideas, ideas and more ideas. If you don't learn how to focus your people, you'll never boost your results.

3. Focus on context, not content.

If you can apply this concept, I truly believe it's the one thing that will make all the difference to your bottom line. Big words, but very true.

Let me give you an example of what I mean. Sam, the fellow I told you about in the Introduction, started out being the leader who did the exact opposite of what I'm suggesting. Because Sam was under tremendous pressure to produce big results in a short period of time, he felt compelled to control every step. He was obsessed with content.

He personally developed the prospect hit list for his salespeople one evening without their input. Sam created the sales process his team would use, and he would get livid if they didn't follow that process to the letter. When one of his folks called to let Sam know how close a deal was to closing, Sam would ask questions about every little detail that salesperson experienced with the customer. He would move into condescending mode when his people didn't handle issues in the exact way he did.

When I asked Sam why he was so obsessed with controlling the content of what his people did, he said, "Jen, I'm the only one who knows how this process works, and unless I stay on their backs every day, they're not going to get the results they want." He didn't have much confidence in his people, did he?

You can see why three of his top folks left so close to the time the company was going public. I don't think many people reading this book would stay in an environment where the leader was so obsessed.

What did Sam need to do instead? He needed to give his people everything to get their job done then get out of their way. That's the difference between context and content. Someone who is focused on content will become obsessed with the tiny details of how the job gets done. A leader who focuses on context sets up an exhilarating experience where the people are jazzed to do the work.

Yes, Sam learned his lesson the hard way. The day after these three people left, Sam and I focused on creating an environment that allowed his people to shine. More times than not, Sam's team ended up coming up with ideas that never occurred to him – and they ended up with some pretty incredible numbers. If Sam had stayed obsessed on controlling the content, he probably would have joined the new venture graveyard.

Imagine yourself as a head coach walking along the sidelines in the midst of a big game. That's what you do as a leader today – hang out on the sidelines. Your people, they're the ones who play the game. Give them the proper field, lighting, uniforms, training and support to win. Then stand on the sidelines and let them play.

Action step

What is missing for your team to get the results you want? Take a minute to review your 90-day goals for the team. What do your people need that they don't have to produce the outcome you want? I encourage you to put this book down and develop a plan to handle this issue for your people. Let them worry about content. It's your job to give them everything they need to shine.

4. Manage your people's perceptions.

I was having lunch with three of my clients who are the leaders at a fast-growing IT consulting firm. They've moved their small company into hypergrowth, and big things are starting to happen for them. I knew they'd have a lot of opinions about chaos, so I asked for their opinions.

We all agreed that every organization needs chaos in order to breed creativity and new ideas. And it's true that many large companies do a much better job of stomping out chaos. As a small company, these three leaders told me they don't put that much attention to chaos. They thrive on sudden changes in their organization, so why let your competitive advantage leave?

Dave, one of the leaders, pointed out that chaos has a perception problem. I was sharing a story about one of my clients who works at a Fortune 10 company, and how frustrated he is with the bureaucracy he lives with every day. As the director of their e-commerce division, Charles' responsibility is to stay on top of all the new technological Internet tools. Yet he had a real problem: his computer wasn't strong enough to handle videostreaming via the web. He filled out the requisition forms to order a new laptop, and it took four months to get the right approvals before he got this new machine. Four months!

Charles told me his company needs more instant response to

what their people need. I couldn't agree more. Yet if you talked to their purchasing department, they'll tell you they can't support that type of chaos, and they need a formalized approval process in place. You see the problem, I'm sure.

On the other hand, in Dave's small company, one of his employees may decide they need a new computer. Rather than filling out a bunch of paper, Dave's employee would send an email requesting a new computer. It would probably take the leadership team four months to decide if the computer was worth the investment – not because it wasn't important, but because buying their staff new computers was one of 50 priorities on their To-Do list. Dave's team member would get a new computer four months later.

Both employees follow the same process to request a new computer. Both employees experience the same wait time. Four months. Yet the employee at the small company would scream that the company is unorganized, chaotic and doesn't have the right systems in place to handle growth. Charles, on the other hand, is screaming that his company moves way too slow and needs to let chaos reign. Same process. Same outcome. Different perceptions.

Your people will view your environment in many different lights. They're going to think what they're going to think based on what happens to them. Make sure you don't get caught up in what they believe to be chaos if that's not reality. It's your job to point out what chaos is good and what chaos actually turns into toxicity.

Action step

Pull your staff into a room and give each group of three or four people a flipchart and markers. Ask them to identify on one page what "chaos" means in the organization. Have them be a specific as possible in determining what adds too much chaos to their work and shifts the balance from exciting to toxic. On the other page, ask them to outline what "sanity" looks like. Again, specific strategies are important here. Then it's your job to pick one idea and make it real in the next seven days. If you're not willing to do something with what they give you, do not do this exercise.

If you have a team that stomps out chaos and needs more of it, the exercise is the exact opposite. Have them brainstorm what prevents chaos from thriving and develop strategies to let some spontaneity grow.

5. Provide all the resources your team needs.

Are you setting up your team to fail?

Don't think you're immune to this issue. This is perhaps the worst problem I see in corporations. There are too many people doing too many jobs who simply don't have the resources they need to succeed.

Cost cutting is an important measure in all organizations. As an entrepreneur, I spend a great deal of time looking at what return on investment I'm getting for each dollar we spend.

Business is about profit, and I'm not here to tell you it's not. It is.

But what I often see is leaders who set up their team to fail by not giving them the resources they need. I'm not only talking about human capital. That lean and mean attitude demands that fewer people get the same if not more done. What I'm also referring to is not giving your people the tools they need to get the job done.

Jamie is a vice-president of public relations for a family-owned advertising agency. She's grown up with the agency, starting as a new account executive and evolving into quite an influential member of the executive team.

When Jamie and I first started working together, we started a list of everything her team needed to blast through the roadblocks they faced. The biggest toleration on that list was the computer system they had to endure. The size of their media database had grown so large and complex, the computers they used to support the data were simply not powerful enough.

Jamie fought for almost two years to get the right computers. An inexcusable time frame in my mind. A good computer costs less than $5,000, and every single time that system crashed (which was every day) one of Jamie's key people would spend 15–30 minutes booting the system back up. Jamie even documented the time her team spent fixing the computer and how much they could earn billing out on client work. That data ended up being some ridiculous number close to 20 percent of their time being spent on computer issues.

I must give Jamie credit for staying in there. I personally never would have lasted with a company who would not support the technology I needed to do a bang-up job. As I worked with her, I reminded myself this is the same company who refuses to pay for cell phones for their people. And their account executives were out of the office 50 percent of the time.

Every single time your people struggle to get the job done, they feel as if the system is working against them. It is. They end up feeling bitter and dissatisfied, and they have one foot out the door. All you're doing is adding to the chaos and frustration by not giving them what they need. Old economy leadership was about encouraging your people to thrive no matter what the circumstances. Leadership today is about giving your people what they need so they can support the speed and intensity that work demands from them.

Action step

I recommend you take the same steps Jamie did to decide what resources your team needs to do their jobs by starting a list. Take the next two weeks to constantly add to this list. Once you've captured everything your team needs, start prioritizing based on which resources will give you the most boost in productivity and/or a solid return on investment. Be sure to share this priority list with your team along with deadlines of when they can expect to have these resources available.

6. Be consistent. It matters.

The best way to build sanity into a chaotic environment is with structure. No, that doesn't give you permission to establish a whole bunch of rules. I want you to go for structure with flexibility.

Yes, I'm talking about habits here. They're hard as heck to start and even harder to maintain. The cold hard fact is unless you build consistency into how you lead, you will never succeed at transforming chaos into sanity.

Years ago, Larry hired a consultant to his staff work more effectively together. Larry owns a real estate company, and he was experiencing conflicts with his key employees. The problem, this consultant uncovered, was Larry didn't take the time to talk to his people. Not in a way that supported their efforts to get the job done. He would rush into their offices with projects that had to be done right then and there. No time to prepare. No negotiating. Larry demanded immediate response.

The new system required Larry to dictate the day's activities and have that tape on his assistant's desk by 8 a.m. She would type out the dictation, and the team would sit down for a daily staff meeting every morning at 8:30 a.m. This daily schedule allowed them to operate at a very intense pace without anything falling through the cracks.

When Larry hired me to be his coach, I was quite impressed

with how this daily meeting schedule supported the team. That was until the system broke down. Larry went on a two-week vacation, and everyone struggled to get back to their daily meetings when he returned. The result? Chaos ruled.

Larry started getting upset because the team was dropping balls on some key issues, but Larry didn't give them the time they needed. His people felt as if they were running around trying to prevent eggs from hitting the sidewalk.

Everything changed with they got back on their daily meeting schedule.

I think every one of us falls into this trap. We have the best intentions to host weekly staff meetings, yet something "more important" comes up, and we get off track. Your people start losing faith in what you have to say. You walk into their offices with a new idea. To your face they say, "Great idea." Behind your back, they say, "Yeah, right. He/she doesn't stick with anything."

If you take a look at any successful company, you will notice that consistency plays a major role in what their successes. When you go to Starbucks, you expect the same consistent quality and service every time. At McDonald's, the hamburgers taste the same in Ohio as they do in Frankfurt, Germany. Coca-Cola bottles are the same shape with the same color red. This same-ness delivers a consistent message to their customers.

Your employees want this from you, too. Never doubt the power consistency has on your people.

Please do not misunderstand and believe I'm suggesting you create a whole bunch of rules. That's not the case at all. Build a framework in which your team operates. Part of that framework is activities that happened at the same time every day, week, month and quarter. Your people need something to depend on when the world is going crazy around them, and it's your job to provide that consistency. It grounds your people and gives them a safe place when they're feeling stressed.

No, no, don't get caught up in having to plan every hour of every day. You're falling back into trying to control the content. What you're going for is structure that allows for customization. You provide the framework, and your people bring high performance to the table.

That means no matter what you have going on, schedule staff meetings at the same time in the same place. Yes, no matter what, it's the same time in the same place. Financial reports are out on the same day of every month. Birthdays are celebrated in the same way, promotions are acknowledged in the same way, new people are welcomed in the same way.

Too many leaders get caught up in rushing from here to there and never taking the time to build the infrastructure. Your people need you to be calm, cool and collected during these crazy times. And they need you to provide consistency so they feel as if they can depend on you. Can they?

You must be brutal in making sure these standards are maintained and followed. If you don't provide the consistency, your people certainly won't. Distraction is the real enemy in today's economy, and these consistent behaviors give your people what they need to deal with the other chaotic situations that show up.

Action step

What consistent activities does your team need? Take a minute to brainstorm a variety of ways you can provide consistency for your team amidst the chaos circling around them. Do you need to institute weekly staff meetings? Daily voicemail messages to the team? Quarterly team meetings in an off-site location? A different way to celebrate accomplishments?

Select one idea that you want to integrate right away. What support are you going to build in to make this a reality? For example, one of the reasons people hire personal trainers is it forces them to work out every day at the gym. Left to their own devices, most people would work out for a few days and then one morning when they woke up tired, there goes their workout program. Not if a personal trainer is waiting at the gym for you!

Who do you need to get involved with your ideas to provide more consistency? Make sure you set up the system so you experience consequences if you don't follow through on your commitment to create new habits. Over time, these activities will become just a part of how you operate at the office.

THE TRUTH ABOUT CHAOS

If dealing with chaos is a major issue in your organization, I think it's time for me to bring you in on a little secret. You're probably addicted to the intensity and excitement.

There are many of us out there who feel more alive when things are moving quickly. We secretly love not knowing what's next. We wait for the next fire to flame so we can jump in and save the day. We enjoy watching our people thrive no matter what the circumstances, and we reward those people who succeed in the most chaotic situations. We even admire leaders who have this capacity to be grace under fire. And yes, sometimes we create chaos so we can watch how people react when so much is hitting the fan.

That may be fine and well for a while, but eventually this chaos catches up to you. Have you ever gone home at the end of the day completely exhausted and ready for bed at 7 p.m.? That's the price you pay by living in chaos 24/7.

By creating so much ruckus, you're forcing your people to work at intense levels, and you're running the risk of burning them out. You could even have a day like Sam when your top three people quit because they don't want to work in the midst of the fire anymore. I was there, and it wasn't pretty.

Tell yourself the truth. Are you addicted to the chaos? If you are, then it's time to get a grip. Do anything – and I mean anything – to bring sanity back into your world.

What you really want at the end of the day is to achieve the right results, inspire your people and make it home in time for dinner. Don't let your addiction to the heart-pounding, fast-moving work environment get in the way of getting what you want. Your people will thank you. And so will I. We need strong leaders to push back and bring sanity back into the workplace.

Are you one of the strong ones?

IT DRIVES THEM CRAZY WHEN . . .

1. You try out too many ideas. They want to know what's important as much as they want you to get out of their way.
2. You only give information on a "need to know" basis. No one likes working in the dark.
3. You knee jerk to solve problems rather than solving them forever.
4. You think chaos is just part of the game. They want solutions, not excuses.
5. You're driving yourself wild with all the intensity, but you're driving them crazy with the same behaviors.
6. You give them too many targets to focus on.
7. You spend most of your time consumed with the details, and you don't let them make their own decisions on how to do the job.
8. You have a different idea of what chaos means – and you don't really care what they think about it.
9. You don't give them all the resources they need to get the job done. You tell them to find a way without sacrificing the goal.

10. You're addicted to the intensity a chaotic organization creates. They know it. And they hate you for it.

IT DRIVES THEM WILD WHEN . . .

1. You make their jobs easier by removing obstacles.
2. You allow them to focus on what truly matters.
3. You create an inspiring game. And it drives them even more wild when you let them play the game the way they want to play.
4. You spend the majority of your time coming up with permanent solutions to the problems they're facing.
5. You give them the long-term vision, but you let them decide how to reach the goals.
6. You're a master at helping them focus on one thing. And the results prove this strategy works.
7. They have everything they need to be brilliant at their work.
8. You understand what the word chaos means, and you reduce the stressors for them.
9. You're committed to breaking your addiction with chaos. They support your efforts to create a saner work environment.
10. You may be sane, but you're never boring. And they love that about you.

CHAPTER #2

Honor your people

I'm warning you right from the beginning: this is going to be a tough chapter to read. I'm going to get in your face to make sure you're not driving your people crazy. Are you?

AS A LEADER, you need to walk the line between driving results and keeping your people happy. Let me be clear before we start: retaining your talent has nothing to do with being handcuffed by them. Too many leaders are afraid to do what they need to do because they're scared to death about losing their key people. I want to coach you to get the results you want while inspiring your people. This is not about walking on eggshells every single day. It is about learning how to maximize the potential of your people.

It's funny, but when I first sat down to write this book, I had "Honor Your People" as step 6 in the seven-point process. I, like many of you, am extremely results driven. At the end of the day (or the month or the quarter or the year), I want to look at my company and see real results: increased revenues, improved customer satisfaction levels, high quality employees and much higher profits. So when I approached the idea of driving results and consistently sending everyone home in time for dinner, the first place to look, I thought, was how to drive the right outcomes. That way no one would feel guilty going home at a decent hour because the important work was done.

But I got halfway through writing this book, and it became clear that unless you can harness the collaborative power of your people, you won't get any results. No matter how much you transform your leadership style, how many programs you implement, new things you try and no matter how much you want to accomplish the big goal, unless you're able to get your people inspired by their work, success will elude you.

The place to start isn't with the results. The place to start is with your people.

IT'S NOT ABOUT TREATING YOUR PEOPLE LIKE FREE AGENTS

Now there are a lot of consultants and authors out there who will tell you that you have to approach your employees as if they're professional athletes. It's a free agent society, and everyone is only in it for themselves, they say. You must treat your talent like an NFL owner would his football players. Pay them high salaries, let them do their jobs and allow them to play for another franchise whenever they decide it's time to go. Oh, and don't forget having to negotiate with their career agents. You're going to have to start a Division for Career Agents Relations pretty soon if you follow their advice.

Yuk. What I think about when I hear this "treat your employees like athletes" is a whole bunch of spoiled employees demanding more perks and making it difficult to get the job done. I keep seeing that scene from the movie *Jerry McGuire* where Tom Cruise is screaming, "Show me the money!"

One of my clients, Gary, a vice president in a fast- growing pharmaceutical company, expressed it best:

> *This is another one of those ideas that sells a lot of books, but fails miserably in real life. When I managed IT, I had some highly skilled "athletes." They could go to work somewhere else any time, and they reminded me of that a lot. I gave them what they wanted most – autonomy – but also the responsibility that went along with that freedom. Just like the 20-year-old athlete who skips the last year in college to make millions in professional sports, my employees didn't know how to deal with it. Their universe evolved around them and the heck to the rest of the business. I eventually cleaned house of them all.*

That's not to minimize the free agent market. There are thousands of employees who would prefer to leave the company and contract their services back to you. As an entrepreneur myself, I completely respect their need to be on their own and you need to as well. My point: stop taking bad advice you're getting by basing your leadership style on professional sports.

What happens to your customers if you treat your employees like star-studded athletes? Look at what's happened in professional sports. Fans have been leaving ballparks and stadiums in droves because they're tired of the greed. They're tired of players and owners only caring about how much money they have to line their pockets. The fans miss the love of the game, and I know many of the players do as well.

That's what your employees truly miss in the business world. They miss the love for the company. They miss adoring you as the leader and doing anything for the good of the team. No, not at the sacrifice of their own lives. They want great work *and* a great life. Most people who work for you long for the days when they used to jump out of bed and rush to the office because they enjoyed being there. Your people want to love their work again. And you as their leader are the one who can bring that love back to the game of business.

Fundamentally, the people who work inside companies typically want to work for someone else. They have a high need for some safety and security – a lot less than twenty years ago, but still a need for a steady paycheck. What they really want is a gracious, caring, compassionate, inspiring leader to guide them to love the work they're doing. You have to realize one key thing: if your employees wanted to be entrepreneurs, they would be. They need you just as much as you need them. And I mean that in a good way, a healthy way. You're in this together, and you can find solutions *together.*

It's time for you as the leader to honor your staff. If anyone's going to bring the love back into the game, it's going to be you.

All great teams start with a great coach, which means it's time to look at how you do the exact opposite of what your people need to perform. What are you doing that gets in their way?

HOW YOU DISHONOR YOUR STAFF

Here comes the hard part. When was the last time you showed your team respect? I mean, deep "I care about you and who you are" respect.

Okay, I know your first reaction was, "Jen, I always show my team respect." I'm not sure I believe you.

When stuff is hitting the fan and you're behind on delivering what you promised, your natural instinct is to throw the "my employees come first" mantra right out the door. Heck, most of us do that every single day. We fundamentally believe that once we produce the result we want, we can go back and take care of our people issues.

There are some of you reading this book who want to respect your team because it's the right thing to do. You were taught to treat other people as you want to be treated, and you try to follow the Golden Rule. This chapter will take what you're already doing well and take your skillset to a whole new level.

And then there are the rest of you. I'm talking to all the hard-driving, director-style, I-really-wish-I-could-be-a- dictator leaders out there. I know what you're thinking. You're saying you'll do anything to get the result you want. What really drives you isn't the people at all. What inspires you is getting the outcome you truly want. In essence, the outcome is a heck of a lot more important than the people involved.

It's okay. You don't have to admit this to anyone but to yourself – and me.

Every day I see leaders who, under stress, act like real schmucks. They think it's acceptable to act a certain way because the results are what matter in a business. And that's exactly what the problem is.

As executive coaches, my coaching team and I typically work with very driven leaders. Founders of companies, CEOs of fast-growing dot-coms, leaders and business owners with tremendous potential to be the best of the best. What they have in common is they produce results. It's their No. 1 priority. They love to get in the game of business and achieve. To sweat it out, tweak the systems and get the right outcomes. They're the type you see at the airport talking on their cell phones as they write in their Palm Pilots waiting for the plane to take off. (And they're typically the one the flight attendants are telling to turn off their phones during take-off.)

Many times on their quest to produce results, they forget to take care of their people. I had a client once who was a huge real estate developer. Fred had started his company in his thirties, and in twenty years he built a huge conglomerate. He was the example of a fabulous rags-to-riches story, a true example of someone who came from nothing and built a very successful company.

There was just one problem: Fred is a horrible leader. If you worked for him, he would expect you to be available 24/7. He thought nothing about calling his people on weekends to talk through a business issue, and he often scheduled evening meetings. If he wanted to work at any hour of the day or night, Fred expected you to be right along with him. He was so obsessed with having his staff be at his beck and call, he even installed a doorbell from his office to his assistant's desk. His executive assistant was supposed to run into his office any time that bell rang. When I asked him why the doorbell, he said he got tired of calling her office on the phone only to get voicemail because she was talking to someone else. (I swear this is a true story.)

Fred was driving his folks so crazy, his executive team was excited to see me come in as his coach. Unfortunately, Fred wasn't interested in making the necessary changes. He couldn't see that he was the one who was causing all the problems. The last thing I heard, a large chunk of his executive team was talking to recruiters.

Take a look at these seven things leaders do to dishonor their staff. Notice how many leaders are unconscious to the subtle ways they tell their people that they aren't important. Are you one of the offenders?

1. **One of your team members is in your office when your phone rings. You answer the phone.**

Warning! Warning! You just sent a clear message to your employee that the phone call was way more important than they are. Unless you told them *before* they started speaking that you were expecting an urgent call you had to take, you put the task before the employee.

The same thing goes for that cell phone. Every time you're with someone and you answer your cell phone, you're dishonoring who you're with. Are you doing this to your spouse? Your kids? Your staff? Your co-workers? The most amazing leaders all do one thing very well: when they're with someone, they're with them. They're present to what's going on in the moment, and they handle phone calls at another time.

It drives your people crazy when you answer the phone when they're with you. Honor your people and turn that phone off.

2. You show up late for meetings.

I have a client who is late for just about everything. Between he and I, it's a big joke when he shows up late with me because I understand the psychology of why he's always late. (And I truly believe he will eventually want to work on changing this.) But you know what? It's not his staff's job to understand why he's doing something. What many of them believe – and deep down, it's true – is he believes that what's going on in his life is more important than their issues. Every single time he shows up late, he's sending a message that they aren't a priority.

Yes, I know. Emergencies happen that push you off track. I'm not talking about arriving late once in a while. I'm talking about being late most of the time. It's easy to forgive someone who shows up late once in a while; it's a real problem when they show up late *every time*. There's something else going on.

You honor your team by being there when you said you would. If that means you need to be the first person in the room, do it.

It drives them crazy when you blatantly show them through your actions that your life is more important than theirs. Please show up on time!

3. **One of your employees has a family emergency or doesn't feel well. You want to show compassion, but what you really care about is getting the work done so you focus on that.**

This seems like an obvious one, but notice how you react when one of your team members needs to take some time off to handle a family crisis. When I talk about honoring your team, I'm not just talking about pretending to honor them. If you want to be a powerful leader, you need to be authentic. Leadership is about people, it's not just about getting the job done.

I saw this happen in my own life with how I treated one of my assistants. I was in a hotel room in Atlanta a few months ago, reviewing my PowerPoint presentation one last time before I went to speak to a large audience. But I had transferred the wrong presentation to my laptop. The one I needed was in two places: my computer at my office and on my assistant's desktop. In two hours, I was going to be standing in front of 300 people. I desperately needed the right presentation.

I called Susan to have her email over the file. No problem, right? Well, here's the kicker. I had spoken to Susan two hours earlier, and she had told me she wasn't feeling well. She was going back to bed. I of course expressed my concerns then, but when my PowerPoint problem came up, I really didn't care if she was sick or not. I needed that file. And fast.

You know what comes next. I called her office number, her cell phone and her home number until I finally reached her. Fortunately for me, the presentation was on her home computer, and I got my file but only after I convinced her this was a real crisis. She needed to get out of bed.

Would I do the same thing if faced with the same situation? No. When I sat back and reviewed what I had done, I was so appalled that we soon hired another administrative assistant who can now back Susan up on these important projects. And Susan backs Julie up. Acting like a real jerk under stress wasn't the answer. My solution was to build a reserve of administrative help so we can cover each other when we need to. Murphy's Law always does at the most inopportune time.

4. **You allow employees with kids to leave early to attend soccer games or school activities. Your single and no-kid employees are expected to burn the midnight oil.**

Ah, so maybe this one hits a little too close to home? Remember having a life is not just about family. You need to honor all your employees, not just those with kids. What about those single employees who have a horse or dog that needs to be cared for? I have six pets, and you'd be surprised how much work – and love – my animals need. Don't assume that because you have employees who are single, they don't have lives. Keep in mind that work doesn't have as much importance as it once did, and many of your employees won't put up with being treated like second-class citizens.

5. **You believe that money will buy their happiness, so you pay them off rather than changing the company culture.**

I was coaching a high potential leader in a large telecommunications company a few years ago who was challenged with this very thing. Gail is the mother of two children, and she was struggling with how to balance her family and her work. Gail was in a very demanding position, and every week she was dealing with a vice president who violated every one of her personal boundaries. She got called into evening conference calls and had to answer weekend phone calls. She was given assignments on Friday and expected to deliver results on Monday. Yet at the same time, Gail couldn't get approval for new staff for her overworked department because "it just wasn't in the budget."

When I asked Gail why she didn't say no and push back, she told me her VP had actually told her that at her salary level, she was expected – no, required – to put work first. It was as if paying Gail a $100,000 a year gave her VP the right to demand where Gail spent her time.

I coached her to have a conversation with the VP about reducing the workload or, better yet, creating an environment that allowed her team to have a life. Rather than deal with the problem, this VP gave Gail a $20,000 raise. I think she really believed if she paid Gail more, Gail would tow the company line and continue working like a dog.

You know what happened next. Gail left her employer of fifteen years to work at a place with a much saner work environment. The way I look at it, that telecommunications company lost one of their huge producers because their leaders believed $120,000 equaled slavery.

I know you've seen this before. An employee threatens to leave because they're unhappy, so you increase their salary and do nothing about the complaints. Fred, the real estate developer I told you about, believed this. He paid his people almost 50 percent more than anyone else in the industry, and for that, he thought he could control their lives. Perhaps you give them more stock options and tell them to focus on the long-term payoff rather than the long working hours. Many leaders believe that money is the answer to retaining their talent. According to Society of Human Resources Managers, 89 percent of corporate managers believe money is the No. 1 factor in keeping their employees at the company.

Sure, you'll keep them around for a while by giving them more money, but you're crushing their spirit in the meantime. They may show up at the office, but they've mentally shut themselves off.

Money is not the answer to keeping your people happy. Powerful leaders understand that people need something more enduring than the promise of instant wealth.

6. **You schedule evening or weekend business event, and you tell your team these events are supposed to be for fun.**

I have clients who schedule team-building activities with their people on the beaches of Hawaii, white-water rafting in Colorado and trips to Arizona spas. They believe that if they would get their people together to get to know each other on a more intimate level, performance would improve.

I've never had any problems with team-building activities. Getting people together in unique locations gives everyone a change of scenery and can open up communications. But the challenge I see is when leaders host these events during non-working hours.

No matter if you're on the beach in Hawaii or doing a team-building ropes course on a Saturday, if it's a required event for your employees, it's still work. Did you hear that? Your people are still working. This isn't free time and for some people, it isn't even fun. If these activities are so important to you, why aren't you taking your team out during the work week? At the very minimum, if you must schedule a weekend event, do you give them time off the next week to make up for taking their free time to focus on work? I didn't think so.

Many people are tiring of constant interaction with their co-workers. They are already working 60-hour work weeks, and they see the same faces day after day. It's impossible to be with your co-workers and not talk about work. Your people want a life, and they're getting sick of spending their so-called free time with their co-workers. They don't care if they're in Hawaii or Colorado. They want time away from the office, and you're invading their personal lives by scheduling weekend activities. What message are you sending by further blurring the lines between work and life?

7. You say things like, "I'm the boss, that's why."

Gosh, I really hope this isn't you . . . this is the old way of leading from a dictatorial point of view. It drives them crazy when you pull rank and act like the boss.

Move into the 21st century, will you?

HOW TO START HONORING YOUR STAFF

Honoring your staff is often a subtle thing. It's related to how you show up every single day and how you treat your people during your good days and your not-so-good days. Here are some specific things you can do to show your staff that you do honor and respect them. I've seen it work with other clients, and it can work for you, too.

1. Think about your people first, the outcome you want to produce second.

Why would you want to put people first and the result second? That's a darn good question. The answer is exactly why I reorganized this book and put "Honor Your People" as step 2 on this seven-step process.

If you don't honor your staff, you won't get the results you want. The bottom line is the more you honor your team, the more likely they are to produce amazing things for you. Your people will do more for you because they love and respect you than they ever will do for a dictator.

Think back to the leaders you adored working for in the past. You would have done just about anything to accomplish what needed to get done. Why? Because you wanted your leader to be proud of you, appreciate you and acknowledge your achievements. They support you, and in return, you wanted to perform for them.

One of my clients said something to me that describes exactly what I'm trying to say. She said, "Jen, I watch my manager in action, and I am in awe of her as a leader. She makes me want to be the best I can be." And this from my client who had recently gone through a difficult company reorganization where she was taken from a role she thrived in to a job that wasn't so hot. She could have left the company in a huff, but she stayed because her manager showed her so much compassion that my client wanted to strive to be the best.

Wow. That's what I want your people to say about you!

Action step

It's your job to put the fun, inspiration and love back into the game of business. To do that this week, I want you to

> start every conversation with your people by asking them how they are, what they're up to, anything about who they are as a human being. That includes asking them how their weekend was, how the dog is, if they won their latest soccer game with their twelve-year-old kid. Many leaders barge into meetings or cubicles to bark out orders rather than taking the time to ask how someone is – and paying attention to the answer. This week practice putting your people first by asking them how they are.

It drives your people wild when you think of them before pushing for a huge goal.

2. Learn what inspires your team. And stop motivating them.

I remember a few years ago one of my clients was highly annoyed during one of our coaching sessions. She was almost to the point of giving up. As a leader, I know you've experienced the same thing. Jane was not dealing with financial issues or client problems. What was annoying her was her employees. She said, "Jen, it's just so unnerving. I try to motivate my people and all they do is roll their eyes are me. They just don't care about this place as much as I do."

Sounds way too familiar, doesn't it?

Every leader I know has faced this problem at one time or another. In order to reach your company goals, you need your staff to rise up to a whole new level. You believe they can do it, but everything you try to use to motivate them just doesn't work. And you're right. They don't care about your business as much as you do.

Maybe you've found yourself in the same place as Jane. Leaders often look outside their staff to find some stimulation in order to get results. They're looking for anything that will get their staff to perform, so you try setting up a big reward when goals are met. Motivational tapes. Negative consequences. But nothing you do to motivate your team works.

What if there is a better way? There is. Stop motivating your people. Instead, you need to harness the power of inspiration.

There's a big difference between motivation and inspiration. Motivation is an external force that pushes, kicks and forces your team to get things done. Like a looming deadline. A fierce boss. The pain of what will happen if they don't do it. Being motivated always carries a big price. It's like a drug that hooks you. The feeling never lasts, and you have to keep going back for more and more motivation. As the leader, you're the one who has to keep going back to drive the team. In my world, that's way too much work for anyone to take on.

Inspiration, on the other hand, is an inner drive that keeps you moving. It's passion on fire. Being inspired stirs your soul, and it stimulates your thinking. When you're inspired, you naturally do the things you need to do. You don't need someone or something else to get you moving. You just do it because it's what you want. Not because you were forced into it.

Motivation carries with it a lot of pain. Inspiration is effortless.

The real question: How do you shift from needing to motivate your team to helping them tap into their own inspiration? It's real simple. Find out what they really want. I don't means as a collective whole, but what jazzes each one of them individually.

That doesn't mean you guess at their reasons or assume you know. You find out. Sit down and talk to your team members one-to-one. Why are they working? What is it about the work that excites them? What accomplishments will make them feel amazingly successful at work?

Once you know what inspires your team on an individual level, you can use that to inspire them. No, not by cattle prodding them, but by reminding them how great they'll feel when they accomplish something big for the right reasons.

Motivation is all about you. Not too many people will work at 110 percent just to please the boss. (Remember how I told you earlier in this book that your employees have lost their awe of leaders?) Inspiration, on the other hand, is about them.

Use what I call the "Levi Straus Syndrome." Remember a few years ago when Levi announced they were going to customize a pair of jeans for any customer who wanted that? We no longer had to go stand in front of shelves and shelves of jeans and decide which style to buy. No longer would we have to try on ten pairs just to buy nothing because not one pair seemed to fit the way we wanted them to. Leadership in today's economy is not about one size fits all. It's about learning what inspires your people individually and designing their work around that.

Action step

This week I want you to sit down with all your team members individually and ask them why they're working. What's the real reason they show up at the office every day? What inspires them to reach higher levels of performance? Then sit back and listen. I mean really listen. You'll find that one person is inspired by the opportunity to make more money. Another will be inspired by flex time, another by recognition for a job well done. And others by things you never even dreamed like being able to create new stuff, be seen as a real expert or to learn something new every day.

Use this information to leverage your staff's performance. The best leaders in the world push the right buttons so their people use their own desires to perform. I didn't say it was your job to push them to perform, but it is your job to know what's in it for them, and then use that to get the work done.

Did you get that? Inspire your people by focusing on what they want, not on what you think they want. Inspiration is not about you, it's about them.

Jane used this approach and increased her team's performance by 50 percent in a twelve-month period. Yes, I did say a 50-percent increase. This stuff works.

You'll drive your people wild if you stop motivating and inspire them instead.

3. Treat them like their your business partners. They are.

Remember that in today's economy, employees are not the same breed that they used to be. Their entrepreneurial spirit is alive and well, and you need to honor that by treating them like real business partners. They no longer work for you; they work *with* you. And there's a huge difference in that.

Let me explain it a different way. I have a client who's a 55-year-old white man by the name of Jack. If you looked at Jack, you'd think he's similar to every other middle-aged white executive out there. For many years, that's exactly who he was. He drives a black Mercedes, has his office on the top floor of his office building full of dark mahogany furniture, and Jack has three administrative assistants who work exclusively for him. The majority of his career was spent climbing the corporate ladder as a dictatorial leader who barked out demands and used fear to get his employees to produce the results he wanted.

For a while, this worked. Until Jack took an assignment to take on the top leadership role in IT.

His old leadership style no longer worked. Jack would bark out commands, and his technical folks who turn their noses up at him. Jack would threaten to fire them, and his top people left for higher-paying jobs in other companies. For the first time in his life, his style of leading wasn't working. And Jack became desperate when his turnover rate hit 50 percent.

That's right about the time I stepped in as his newly hired executive coach. One thing about Jack is he's a fun guy to be around – when he wants to be. He's always been the type of executive who builds great relationships with a company's suppliers. He knows how to put together a strategic alliance, how to build long-term relationships and how to create win–win experiences for everyone involved. My question: why wasn't he using those skills with his people? He told me he didn't see his people as suppliers at all. They worked for him, and there was something different in how you treat an employee verses how you treat a vendor.

Now you can see where Jack went off track. Your employees won't stand for this anymore. And neither did Jack's.

The first thing Jack and I did was change his definition of who his people were and what they meant to him. No longer were they employees, they were his partners. Think about that: how you communicate changes when you treat your people like partners. What you share with them changes, how you inspire them changes, how you reward them changes. Jack needed his people to perform as much as they needed him to lead. But it wasn't until he changed his leadership style to treat his employees as his partners that everything improved.

Jack's story is a success, that's for sure. After the first twelve months of working with me, Jack stopped the massive employee exodus and was building a team of folks who adored him as much as he adored them. All because he changed how he viewed their role in his life.

Action step

Take a few minutes this week to decide what you can do differently to treat your employees as if they're your business partners. Is it time to share the financials with them? Do you need to have a heart-to-heart conversation on where the business is really going and how much you need their help? Is it time to bring them in on key decisions before you make up your mind? Do one thing differently this week to show your employees they truly are your partners in reaching the company's long-term goals.

4. Be caring and compassionate. And be willing to help.

I watched an incredible leader at work recently, and I'm still touched by the experience. I was catching a flight from Dallas to Atlanta as I was in the middle of a week-long business trip. It was the end of the day, and everyone on the plane was ready to get home. You could see it in their eyes. I had just settled into reading a magazine I'd been carrying with me for four days, when I saw a gentleman come out of the first class cabin to talk to a woman sitting in front of me.

He was probably 35 years old, and he had this gentle way about him. He was carrying his cell phone on his waist and holding his ear piece in his hand. You could tell he had a lot going on in his life – he just had that look – but you wouldn't know it by his presence.

It turns out this woman works for him, and he wanted to know how she was planning to get home once their plane landed. She told him her husband was picking her up at the airport.

The coolest thing happened that caused me to stop reading and pay attention. He said, "Why don't I drop you off? I have a car service waiting for me when we land, and it'll save your husband a trip through that horrible traffic. You've worked so hard on this trip for me. It's the least I can do."

He proceeded to ask her if she had a cell phone, and when she said her battery was dead, he immediately called the husband on his phone. You should have seen her face during all this. He was making her feel like a queen, and she was touched by his kindness. So was I.

When was the last time you saw a leader be so gracious and polite? This guy went out of his way to take care of his employee. He took the time to get out of his seat to offer a kind gesture, something he didn't have to do. Yes, it probably took him longer to get home by offering to drop her off, but he didn't seem to mind. Of course I have no idea if she just closed a huge account or if she saved a disheartened customer. Here's what I do know: this is a leader who really cares about his people.

It's one thing to talk about taking care of your team, but it's quite another to actually do it. When was the last time you went out of your way to do something kind for one of your staff members? Ah yes, I know. It's been a long time. That's the real problem in our crazed, fast-paced world. We forget to invest the energy to let people know how much we honor and appreciate them.

I'm guilty of this more times than I care to admit. I sometimes get so charged up to delegate a task that I fail to ask my staff how they're doing. Instead, I jump right into the projects that have to be completed. (Go on, you can admit you do the same thing.) There are times when my calendar is so jammed, I cut off conversations to rush off to something else. (Yeah, like you've never done that before.) Other times I forget to say thank you for a job well done. Or give a special something just to say how much I appreciate their effort because I'm already off focused on something else. (Sounds familiar?)

You know, this behavior can be found in long-term marriages as well as showing up with your team. When you're with someone every single day, it's easy to take them for granted. It's easy to think you'll make it up to them when things aren't so hectic or busy. The next thing you know they're leaving for something "better," and you wonder why.

What this guy reminded me was how powerful a kind gesture can be. It's often the little things that matter the most, but it's almost the little things we fail to do.

One quick point: I told this story once when I was speaking in front of a group of leaders. The human resources person came up to me afterwards and told me this leader set himself up for a sexual harassment lawsuit by extending this kind of gesture. She wasn't there to watch this situation unfold, and I disagreed with her comment. But isn't that a sad commentary about today's world that we even need to worry about these things?

I mention this point only because in today's litigious environment, you need to be extra careful. Extend a kind gesture, and be gracious to your staff, just don't put yourself in a compromising situation.

Action step

During the next few days, focus on doing one nice thing for each member of your team. It could something as little as holding the door open for someone who has their hands full. You could choose to stay late to help with a big mailing or arrange to have groceries delivered to their homes as a thank you because they're burning the midnight oil on a hot project. Extend a kind and gracious gesture this week and watch the reaction. Your team will either be touched by your kindness or they'll be so shocked, they'll wonder what you're up to. Either reaction is the step in the right direction.

You'll drive your people wild when you extend a kind hand to them.

5. Celebrate their successes. A lot.

I have had the great pleasure of coaching two wonderful leaders who work in a fast-growing Internet company. (Yes, one of the survivors.) Al and JoAnn were responsible for launching a new division at their company. As with every start-up, Al and JoAnn faced many challenges on this journey, least of all tremendous pressure from the CEO to produce large revenue numbers so the company could go public twelve months later. Like so many of you reading this book, they were up for the challenge. They worked their butts off – and pushed their team to get the right results.

A lot of things went wrong as they were working to reach their goals, but a lot of things also went right. At the end of one particularly amazing quarter when the team generated revenues at 180 percent over quota, Al and JoAnn decided they needed to celebrate their successes. They both dressed up in black tie attire and went to the office to begin the celebration.

Some of their team members were spread out all over the country, but they arranged for each person to get a bottle of champagne in the mail. They had everyone call in to a conference call where they simultaneously popped open their champagne and toasted their successes. They also included a gift certificate to a hoity restaurant in their employees' cities, and they arranged dinner reservations for their employees and a guest that evening. Yes, each employee was treated to a fabulous dinner in their own city. This was not an easy feat as there were fourteen employees in different cities, but was it worth it? I'd say it was.

There's nothing like strutting around in formal attire and drinking champagne to make you feel incredibly successful. Al and JoAnn know how to play hard, and they know how to celebrate (when they give themselves permission to do it).

They, like you, are so focused on driving results they sometimes forget to relish their accomplishments. This time they celebrated the right away. For the right reasons.

When was the last time you celebrated with your team? When was the last time you went up to someone who is putting in the extra effort and acknowledged who they are?

The real question: Why don't you celebrate more?

What I see most leaders do is take their accomplishments for granted. It's as if they forgot how much effort it took for their team to achieve a big feat, and they've already moved on to the next goal. I know you do that in your own life, and here you are doing the same thing to your people.

As human beings, we need to time to celebrate. Just as football players celebrate a Super Bowl win, you must do the same thing with your people. There's nothing worse than working for a leader who only focuses on the negative behaviors rather than the positive ones. Celebration is one of best ways to keep your talent fulfilled – and ready to tackle the next big goal.

Action step

What are you going to do to let your team revel in their successes? Sit down and make a list of twenty-five things you can do to celebrate with your team. Go on. Just pull out a piece of paper and come up with twenty-five ways you can create excitement for a job well done. Better yet, ask your staff what they think at your next staff meeting.

You'll drive your people wild if you take the time to celebrate their accomplishments.

6. Give up your need for control.

Being a control freak has its advantages. Okay, maybe not for the people around you, but certainly for you. Most control freaks I know – and many of them happen to be my clients – have achieved tremendous results in their lives. Control freaks are often the ones we admire because they have accomplished such amazing things. They're the ones who rise to the occasion in the middle of a crisis, take command and produce outstanding results. They set themselves up to be the hero, and every time, they deliver.

Yes, control freaks produce results, but in the quest for high performance, there comes a time when control no longer works. One of my clients, Jane, positioned herself in a fast-growing company to become the leader of a new division. All of a sudden, Jane was not just a producer anymore. She had a staff to manage and inspire, and Jane soon discovered that she can control herself and her environment, but she couldn't control her people. Not really anyway.

She discovered this fact the hard way when her department was required to produce a ridiculously high revenue number one quarter. No, not because the company truly needed these revenues in such a short timeframe, Jane was trying to prove to the CEO that she could perform in this new role. She herself set the high number. It was her first time in such a powerful leadership position.

Jane's team wasn't yet in place and those that were on board weren't properly trained. But the pressure was on. Rather than negotiate reasonable deadlines, Jane took it upon herself to produce the result. I mean *almost exclusively by herself*. She blew off everything that didn't have to do with signing contracts with new customers. She worked like a dog for three full months to get the job done. Like all control freaks, Jane pulled it off. She reached that ridiculously high revenue goal, but she paid the price with damaged work relationships, employee turnover and a sick feeling that things had to change.

When Jane and I were discussing this situation after it was over, I pointed out that her need for control got in her way of building the right team. She asked me, "What's wrong with being a control freak? I got the results, didn't I?" That's really a normal reaction because as I've said before, controlling the situation gives you a feeling of power and success.

You rely on your own abilities, and you know that you can pull a rabbit out of the hat if you need to. You just can't trust or expect anyone else to do that, so it's always up to you. You also know that the reason you are successful right now is because you've learned how to set up the game so you win. And win you do. So why would you want to give that up? Jane had a good pint.

As a recovering control freak myself, I understand more than you'll ever know. As I told Jane, when you're so focused on controlling everything around you, you rip the joy right out of your life. How can you be happy with the burden of responsibility you have to carry? How can you be joyful when you

have the work of five people to do? How can you find fulfillment when you have so darn busy doing the work you don't
have time to experience satisfaction?

But the real kicker isn't that you won't have joy in your life.
For a control freak, the true indication of success is not in the
joy, it's in the results. The real kicker is what got you to where
you are today won't get you to where you want to go. Did you
get that? If you want to produce results as a leader, you must
give up your need for control.

Think about it this way. As a high performer, do *you* enjoy
working for a control freak? Are you inspired by someone
who micromanages? No, of course not. Well, neither is your
staff. If you don't learn to give up your need for control, you
will lose all your high performers, and you won't get the
results you want from your team as they're purposefully sabo-
tage the results just to get back at you. Worse, you will have to
carry the burden of responsibility for everything the rest of
your life. If there's one thing I know, deep down inside, control freaks want someone to jump in and help.

It's time for you to give up that darn ego. I know, you hate this,
but it's true. When your ego is in the way, you actually start to
believe that you're the only one who can do something. Give
me a break. This is your inflated ego talking. If you want to
break your issues with control, give up the ego. You can't be a
strong, powerful leader if you're walking around believing
you're the only one with the answers. The truth is there are
people out there who actually have a cool insight or two that
would dramatically increase your results if you would just lis-

ten. And in today's economy, most of your staff actually know more than you do.

But on the other hand, honor your need to control. Yes, that means that you (1) admit you're a control freak, and (2) set up a system to get that need fulfilled. Let me give you an example from my own life. When I delegate a project, there are many things that happen between the time I hand off the project and when the result comes in. The problem is I personally obsess about all the little things that have to happen to produce the results. My mind is filled with all the details until the result shows up. Knowing this about myself, I could allow myself to obsess about these things or I could set up a weekly meeting with my staff to go through the list of projects completed, projects in process and projects needed to be completed. I do the later most of the time. This check-in process allows me to show up once a week and get my need for control fulfilled. The rest of the week my staff works as they normally would.

If you have the need for control, let yourself get this need fulfilled once a week. Or once a day. Just don't hover over your people every darn minute until they do exactly what you want them to do. Build a system that gives you the details you need without driving your staff mad.

You'll drive your people wild if you stop doing their work for them and instead allow them to step up to get the job done.

Action step

What I'm asking you to do is give up most of what you know and try on something entirely different. Often, you're trying to control things that truly don't matter, so this week, focus on giving up control on the unimportant activities. Sit down right now and make a list of all the results that matter to you. Like memos that go out without typos, customers who must be called back within eight hours, files prepared and one your desk twenty-four hours before you're meeting with a client, whatever.

Then take a look at your to-do list and give up control on something that truly doesn't matter. I don't care what it is, but give it to one of your employees to complete. Even if the result isn't what you wanted, resist the temptation to jump in and save the day. Focus instead on inspiring someone to produce at the same level we both know you can do. It's the only way.

7. Be their coach, not their manager.

One of the single best ways to keep your employees performing is to act like a coach rather than a manager. What do I mean when I say be a coach? It means you see the potential in each one of your people, and you tell them any time that you can that you believe in them. It means you help them get out of their own way, to stop sabotaging their success. In other words, you coach them be the best they can be even if that means you coach them out of the organization.

How will this help you reach your company goals? That's a great question. In today's economy, imagine your team as if you're a coach does when facing his basketball team. This is not about football where the coach calls the shots and the players execute. It's more like basketball.

Traditionally, American businesses operated like a football team. In football, you'll find narrow specialization: linebackers, centers, tackles, running backs, even special teams. Yet basketball puts special emphasis on generalized skills with specialized areas of expertise. Everyone on the court has to dribble, pass, rebound and shoot. A lot like successful business teams.

In football, the team regroups after every play to listen to one player (usually the quarterback) and the coach dictate what's going to happen next.

In basketball, the game is too dynamic to regroup after every shot. Basketball players keep playing and improving as they go along. The basketball team approach is much more effective in today's economy. You need the team members to have general skills, learn as they go and improve the more they practice.

And yes, all great teams need great coaches. That's where you come in.

The reason coaching works in our world today is your employees want autonomy, independence and the ability to chart their own courses. Managing your people is about you – what you can do to get them to do what you need them to do. Coaching your people is about them – guiding them to do what they need to do to get the results they want. And ultimately, you get what you want if you play the game right.

There's a lot of material out there talking about how powerful coaching is as a way of managing your people. It's important to know you will not increase your results by adding a few coaching skills to your toolbox. Learning to listen, challenge and empower your people is simply the first step to leading in today's economy. You need to go beyond using coaching skills and attempt to show up every single day as a coach to your people. I mean a real coach to them.

As a professional executive coach, I obviously know a lot about this topic. Leaders have paid me for years to be their personal coach – and they've often brought my coaching team in to work with their leaders. I've seen just about every situation you can image, and I'm shocked at the things people call coaching. There's a certain art form to being a coach. You need to search out what's brilliant about each one of your people and leverage those strengths in the marketplace. (More on that in Chapter 5.) You must help your people sort through what matters and what doesn't so they can see focus no matter what's going on around them (Chapter 3).

A great coach sets up accountabilities and simple structures people can follow in order to maximize their productivity and results (Chapter 3). Great coaches know when to push their people and when to let them rest (Chapter 4), and they know what to say to make it all okay (Chapter 6). And don't forget, great coaches know when to send their star players home in order to get their heads out of the game for a while (Chapter 7).

Yes, I'm going to teach you in the rest of this book how to be a masterful coach to your people so they find lasting fulfillment being on your team while you together create winning results.

It drives them wild when they have a coach is in their corner when the good stuff shows up – and when the not so great things appear.

Action step

The next time you talk to one of your employees, take a few minutes to ask them how things are coming along. Then step back and listen for what they have to say. I don't mean listen to what words they use. You need to listen to the spirit behind the words. Is this person happy, excited, bummed out or bored? What is their body language tell you about what's really going on?

Powerful coaches have the capacity to figure out the underlying truth about their people and then they use this to get higher performance levels. What does this person need from you to be spurred to reach a new level? That's what I want to communicate to them. Be the coach who tells them you believe in them. Then step back and watch what happens.

FINAL STEPS TO TAKE

If you're truly serious about honoring your people, then sit down right now and make a list of all the ways you think you honor your people. Write down every specific thing you do or have done that shows your people how much you respect who they are. You may even want to brainstorm with other members of your management team to make sure you have a complete list.

Type up the list and send it around to your employees. Ask them to rate how important that action is to them on a scale of 1–5. Five means that behavior is crucial for them feeling as if you want them on the team. One means they can live without that item without it impacting their performance. Do they really feel as if you honor them by engaging in that behavior?

What I often see is a big gap between what you think is important and what your people truly want. The only way to know if disconnection exists in your organization is to take the time to compare notes. What improvements can you make to let your people know you truly honor their place on the team?

THE TRUTH ABOUT HONORING YOUR PEOPLE

The real reason you must honor your staff is because of who you'll become as a person by doing that. What you learn from the people around you makes you an incredible person let along a great leader. It forces you to expand and grow just when things are starting to get a bit dull. My clients have told me many times they were getting bored being the star performer so they decided to move into management. There goes that boredom right out the window!

Putting people first requires that you step out of the way, put your ego aside and focus on the things that truly matter. Caring about the people on your team adds more richness to your life than you'll ever imagine. And yes, it'll produce tremendous results.

This has definitely been true in my own life. I started my business as a sole proprietor, and I was determined to build a business for myself, by myself. That do-it-yourself attitude was what I thought being a business owner was all about. As I look back, I know I was impacted by my husband Steve who started his business when he was 23 years old. I remember being so envious of him. He didn't have to fight traffic, and he didn't have a boss to report to. He could wear his pajamas to his office and not shower until noon if he chose to do that. I loved that Steve didn't have any hassles or frustrations from other people. (I totally missed the point that he had very demanding clients to work with every day . . .)

So I started my business as a sole proprietor, first as a consultant and then as an executive coach. I honed my area of expertise, focused on doing a darn good job for my thriving client base, and for a few years, I loved being on my own. I enjoyed being the expert and being able to do my own thing on my terms.

Then one morning, I woke up bored. Really bored. I was tired of working by myself. I missed the camaraderie of other people, the liveliness that shows up when you're part of a team. My clients were terrific, but working with them wasn't enough for me. I wasn't like my husband who is perfectly happy working in his office all by himself. I wanted to create a real impact on the business world, and there was no way I could do that all by myself. Add to that feeling that I had more business than I knew what to do with, and I decided to start a coaching company. Yes, add people into the mix.

I had the same feeling you had when you became a manager. We were going to create something great as a team.

Whew. Being a leader of people has been one of the most challenging things I've ever done. There are still days when I want to scream and say, "Can you just put aside your opinion and blindly follow me?" Every manager I know has that secret wish. There's a part of us who wants to be the dictator who has a group of people blindly following. Okay, so maybe it's a fantasy, but every leader I know has this fantasy at one point in their careers.

I've made just about every mistake a leader can make including being much more interested in the outcome than how my people felt about the experience. I soon discovered through a series of huge mess-ups that unless I put them first, I would never reach the goals we had set. Never.

Putting my people before the result has taught me more about myself than anything I've ever done. It's taught me that just because I'm the owner of the business (the leader), I don't know much of anything. It's taught me how to be flexible, compassionate, caring and graceful. It's taught me how to put aside my ego and let other people shine. And it's taught me how to swallow my pride and admit more times than I care to remember that I was wrong.

You could say I'm a much stronger person now than I was

when I was working alone. Our company results have been phenomenal, but my own personal growth is the real gift in this.

Which is why *you* must learn how to honor your people. When you're so caught up in producing a certain result and not thinking about your people, you miss a wide range of opportunities. You miss the chance to maximize new market conditions, new ways of leading, new strategies that harness the talent of your people, and you miss what you most need to learn. That doesn't mean that you give up your goals and only focus on keeping your people happy. Don't be ridiculous. It means you look to learn from your own experience and evolve as a human being.

That deep in your heart learning is what I believe leadership is truly all about.

IT DRIVES THEM CRAZY WHEN . . .

1. You answer the phone when you're supposed to be in a meeting with them.
2. You show up late. For everything.
3. You don't respect their opinions.
4. You say one thing and do the other.
5. You're more interested in the result than you are about them.
6. You're a real jerk and don't have a compassionate bone in your body.
7. You use the "one size fits all" way of leading your team.
8. You try to motivate them rather than help them discover their own inspiration.

9. You only focus on what has to get done and not what was accomplished.

10. You let your ego get in the way.

IT DRIVES THEM WILD WHEN . . .

1. You listen to what they have to say.

2. You pay attention to them and prevent distractions from invading your time together.

3. You show up on time. Almost every time.

4. You care more about them than you do the results. And yes, your team still achieves great things.

5. You manage individuals first, the team second.

6. You take the time to solicit feedback – and you listen to what they have to say.

7. You act more like a coach than you do a manager.

8. You find out what inspires them. And you do. A lot.

9. You set aside your ego to do what's best for your people.

10. You know what it takes to be a leader, and you do your best every day to be someone they want to follow.

CHAPTER 3

Maximize productivity

Please do not tell me your problems would be solved if your team would get more done.

Our corporate environments are full of people who believe you need to get more done in order to produce better results. Time management classes are constantly being offered to employees. Use of Palm Pilots and computer schedulers are on the rise. You think that if you would only be more productive, get more done in less time, then you'll finally feel the fulfillment and satisfaction that eludes you. Or you believe if your staff would only follow common-sense time management techniques, you'd all be able to make it home in time for dinner.

GIVE ME A BREAK. Getting more done is not your problem. You and your team already doing more with less. You've taken the seminars, read the books, learned how to use your Palm to prioritize the To-Do list. You're getting more and more done, but feeling less and less satisfied. It doesn't make any sense, does it?

Ask yourself this question: When you go through a whole list of To-Do items, do you feel fulfilled at the end of the day? No, of course not. Why? Because your desk is suddenly full with a whole new pile of crap that needs to get done. The truth is in today's sped-up-I-wanted-it-yesterday world, you're never caught up.

It's even worse for your staff. At least you as the leader have the capacity to delegate work to your team. Many of the folks working for you are just that: the people who do the work. If you think your plate is full, imagine walking in their shoes for a few hours. Many of you already have which is one of the reasons you decided to move into management. You wanted to escape that world.

Maximizing productivity within your organization comes down to this one idea: Do less to achieve more. This seems like a complete paradox to increasing productivity and performance, but it's not. The way to produce the results you want is to actually let some projects go.

Let me share with you an example of why this concept is so powerful.

Rich, one of my clients, was the director of e-commerce at a large Fortune 50 company. In that role, he and his team were responsible for taking a 100-year-old brand marketing company and bringing it into the age of the Internet. Yes, talk about a big job. Not only did they need to look at the impact of change in US markets, but they also needed to incorporate international markets in their daily responsibilities. Their list of things To-Do was huge. And it kept getting bigger.

Rich originally hired me to help him get a life. At that time, he had a young child at home, and his wife was beginning to complain that she didn't see him enough. But the real reason he called me was he was beginning to become very inefficient. Rich is the type of guy that if he promises to deliver a result, he follows through before he promised it to you. It is not unusual for you to get three or four follow-up emails from him explaining where he's at in the process. Rich is not the type to procrastinate or put things off. He's action oriented.

There are times for even the best when things get off track. When Rich became a client a few years ago, this was one of those times. He – and his team – were drowning in all that had to get done. He originally hired me to help him increase his productivity, to get more done in less time.

Once he and his team implemented my ideas and strategies – which I'll share with you in just a minute – they were living the do less to achieve more philosophy. Their results went through the roof. Rich secured a 45-percent raise. They were travelling less, redesigned how their work environment was set up and maximizing individual productivity. No, not by getting more done. By giving 100 percent of their time and attention on the things that matter the most. Do what matters became their mantra.

So what did I coach them to do that made such a huge difference? They started using three key concepts. They are:

1. The Power of Three
2. The Power of No
3. The Power of Theme Days

THE POWER OF THREE

The way to produce results both in your company is to let the power of momentum work for you. In our sped-up-I-wanted-it-yesterday world, distraction is the real enemy. What that means is you're probably pulled in too many directions so you never allow momentum to kick in. Instead you're jumping from one thing to another to another. Yes, it's exhausting. And eventually it catches up with you.

Focus ultimately comes down to identifying the three most important things you do and then spending 80 percent of your time doing them. That's what I call harnessing the Power of Three.

Anyone at any time can put energy behind three things and get the results they want. Three projects. Three big ideas. When you really put your passion behind three things, amazing results show up. You start to build momentum that allows you to get results faster than you do when you're juggling a multitude of things. Momentum is the key here, and it's a vital part to reaching your goals in the allocated amount of time.

Right now you're probably acting as if the items on your To-Do list are supposed to be checked off by the end of the day, but have you taken any time to make sure you have the right things on the list?

Really think about that. How many things are you personally focused against right now? Go on. Make a list. Think of all the projects, all the efforts, all the areas you're trying to get done. Yes, that includes things like attending meetings, reading email, opening your mail as well as what your real job is all about.

Then take it one step further. What are the outcomes your staff is trying to accomplish? Gosh, it's no wonder you're not getting the results you want. Not one of you are spending enough time on the things that truly matter. You're scattered, unfocused and off track.

The Power of Three is the ultimate in concentration of power. You are more powerful if you're able to concentrate and put targeted energy into what you're doing. If you're juggling more than three important projects or priorities, you're bound to forget something – and it's usually something important. So you decide you need to start a list of all the stuff you need to remember, and then you lose the list. Or you put the list on a post-it note, and you just can't seem to find where you put it. Worse, you keep moving the same electronic To-Do list to the next day and then next day and the . . .

When you focus on the three most important things, there's little chance you'll forget what you're doing. You free up time and space to develop strong enhancements to your work that you simply would have missed otherwise. If you don't focus, you won't be able to give 100 percent of your effort, and you dramatically reduce your chances for success.

Your people also need to get clear on the things that truly matter so they can spend 80 percent of their time on the things that will bring the best results. And you're the one who can help them.

Let me share with you how much impact this can have. When I first met Matt, he had flown to Kansas City (where I live) after spending some intensive work days in Europe. He took an all-night flight from London to Chicago and then caught the 7 a.m. flight to Kansas City the next morning. He was drinking cup after cup of coffee during our first meeting, and the stress was noticeable on his face.

Matt hired me because he wanted to get a life and not sacrifice his career in the process. At that time, he was the vice president of business development for a dot-com based in Silicon Valley. Matt was in the process of launching a new division that meant huge revenue dollars for the company. If he and his team didn't produce, the price of their stock when they went public wouldn't be worth anything. The pressure was on.

Before I go any further with this story, you need to know that Matt is one brilliant guy. He has this amazing capacity to see what the future holds before anyone else, and he's able to develop key strategies to bring companies into a new way of operating. His "do anything to get it done" attitude had typically produced tremendous results.

The problem was Matt was paying a huge price for those results. He was losing key employees, working 80 hours a week and getting on the rest of the executive team's last nerve. Yet the reality was he needed to figure out a way to build an infrastructure – fast. He needed to staff up quickly, secure lucrative deals, train his team to pull in more dollars and continue developing the overall strategy for his department. And Matt had about 90 days to do it.

Yes, I know. This was quite a challenge working with Matt and his situation. Everything you've heard about dot-com companies is true. I've worked with many in the last few years, and they work at an intensity you can't imagine unless you work there.

What I coached Matt to do was to gain control over the overload by stepping back and identifying his three priorities. You need to understand that when I talk about the three most important priorities that doesn't mean your focus areas for that day or that week. We're talking the big picture here. What were the three main areas Matt needed to produce results in? What were the areas he needed to put attention in order to get the outcomes he needed?

We ended up calling it the three Ps: *Process, Partners* and *People*. Once we identified the three most important focus areas, Matt could easily execute against them. He put together an action plan of what to do that week in each of his focus areas. He took the Power of Three one step further and started using it to prioritize every day. This strategy forced Matt had to choose what was most important to build the infrastructure necessary to deliver the right results in the shortest amount of time. Up to that point, he didn't want to choose. He was too focused on the activities that had to get done rather than pulling the activities apart and doing what matters.

What's also great about this strategy is Matt was was able to say no to everything that didn't fall into his three focus areas.

What happened next? You guessed it. Matt built his team, got huge results, move the department under a strong manager, and he's since moved to another company to start the building process all over again.

The story doesn't stop there. When Matt decided to leave the first company he was working for – he felt as if he did all the work there he needed to do – he took a job to do pretty much the same thing: build a department from scratch. The last time I saw him, we were having dinner together in San Francisco, and I was particularly interested in how he was handling the sheer volume of work in his new role. He had been on the job about three weeks, and I was curious if he would repeat the same mistakes. We're human, after all.

Matt shared with me his strategy on identifying his three focus areas and how his team was executing against them. There was a sense of calm in his voice, so much different than the first time I met him. I knew Matt and his team would accomplish everything they set out to do.

I sat there with a smile on my face that night. Would you love to be calm, cool and collected rather than scattered and unfocused? Yes, you can see why I was smiling. This strategy works.

Action step

The first step in using the Power of Three is identify what your top three focus areas need to be. Take the time to do this brief exercise.

What are the three most important things you can do – the three things that would matter the most to your company and/or your employees? Write them down here:

1.

2.

3.

Does one of these focus areas have anything to do with removing obstacles or building the right environment for your people? If your list doesn't include this, go back to Chapter 1: Transform Chaos into Sanity. You need to re-read that chapter so you can integrate new ideas into your daily work.

Before you move on, take a few minutes to make sure the three activities you wrote down will help you achieve the 90-day goal you established on page 18. There's no reason to try on a new strategy if you're not willing to tie it into your overall company results. Will focusing on these three areas give you the results you want? If the answer is yes, you have the right Power of Three. If the answer is no, step back and decide what areas need your attention so you accomplish what you've set out to do.

Under each focus area, you need to decide what one thing you can do to get the right results in each of the areas. Good. Now take it one step further. What are the three things you can do this week to achieve results in these areas? What are the three things you can do this month? What about this quarter? This year?

Spend 80 percent of your time on these three things. I know it seems simple but try it. You'll be amazed by how much you get done that truly matters.

THE POWER OF THREE WITH YOUR TEAM

You can immediately – right now – do the same exercise with your team. Here are the steps to follow to integrate the Power of Three throughout your department or company.

Step 1: Your 90-day goal
In the introduction to this book, I asked you to identify a 90-day goal for the work you're doing in this book. Now's the time to pull out that goal and take a look at it. This is the focal point for your Power of Three work with your people.

Step 2: What's on the plate
Pull your team in a room, and ask them to bring a list of every single thing they're working on right now. If they don't arrive with this list already completed, give them the time to make the list before you move on to step 3. It's important that your

people look at every outcome that they're supposed to be working on during the next three months. Even activities like responding to email and attending company events should be on their lists.

The point is to get every person to identify what's on their plate. Until we know what's there, how do we determine what's truly matters?

For a little bit of fun, bring paper plates to your meeting and ask your team to write on the plate what they're supposed to be working on during the next 90 days. This visual representation is incredibly powerful to helping people understand why they feel overloaded. They are.

Step 3: Determine Power of Three areas

Repeat the same process you took yourself through and have each person identify their three most important activity areas. What areas do they need to spend 80 percent of their time in order to produce the results they were hired to do? You're going to need to guide them through this process so you all agree on what their Power of Three activities are.

Step 4: Tie individual performance to the goal

Your team's individual performance must tie back into this 90-day goal or it won't happen – and you're setting yourself up to fail. Once you've determined what you want the team to accomplish (that's your job), then it's time to help each person understand their role in achieving the result.

Take out a big flipchart of paper. On the left-hand side of the page, write down the name of each person on your team. In the middle of the page, write down each of these people's Power of Three focus areas. On the right-hand side of the page, write down the three activities each employee needs to accomplish on in order to achieve the team's 90-day goals. Again, you'll need to work with your people so you both agree on where they want to spend their time.

A word of caution: Great leaders give their people the framework, and then they get out of the way and watch magic happen. In this case, the framework is the 90-day goal you want to achieve and the process to come up with their Power of Three. Let your people tell you what's most important to getting the job done. They know the answers.

If you have a small team, pull out a pen and do this activity right now by yourself. You'll find a great worksheet below to help guide you through this process. Or try out the strategy with three of your key employees. It'll be interesting to see if your team comes up with the same answers you do.

POWER OF THREE EXERCISE

Employee's name	Focus areas	90-day activities
1.	1.	1.
	2.	2.
	3.	3.
2.	1.	1.
	2.	2.
	3.	3.
3.	1.	1.
	2.	2.
	3.	3.

YOUR RESISTANCE TO USING THE POWER OF THREE

Every time we introduce this concept to our clients, we typically get some resistance. Are you thinking these things, too?

1. You're afraid to choose.

For anyone who's open and flexible, the Power of Three can seem stifling. You like to seek out new opportunities, and you like to keep your hands in a lot of things. I completely respect and honor that in you. I'm the same way. I love anything that's hot and new. I'm easily jazzed by anything that can help me get closer to my goals in an easier or more exhilarating way. I like to look for ways to integrate everything. Why not take on dramatically growing my business, moving to a new city, buying a new house that needs decorating and gardening work, starting a major new exercise program, writing a new book and still taking three vacations? Yes, that describes what I added into my life in one twelve-month period.

Here's what I also know: You can do everything you want, just not at the same time. Well, maybe that's not exactly true. You can do everything you want at the same time, but you don't be masterful in anything. And you'll end up pretty darn tired at the end.

That's my entire point. Unless you choose where you want to put your attention, you run the risk of only getting so-so results. We both know you want amazing performance, so bite the bullet and choose. What areas do you need to spend 80 percent of your time to get the results you want?

I'm giving you three different areas to work on. That should keep you entertained for a while.

2. You're afraid you'll miss something if you focus on three areas.

The ol' "I don't want to be left behind" routine rears its ugly head. There are too many opportunities in our world these days. I've been having many conversations with my clients on how to handle hypergrowth in their businesses or careers. Phones are ringing off the hook, email is piling up and calendars are jam packed with high-powered meetings. In a way, this is a good problem to have. It means you're offering something that people want, and they're knocking down the doors to get to you.

What often happens is my clients get stuck on what to do with all the opportunities coming at them. No, they aren't stuck because they can't handle them. They're frozen because the possibilities are so enticing. If they go one way, they'll be amazingly successful. If they take another path, they will also have tremendous success. One of my clients described it best last week. When I asked him how he was, he said, "Dazed and confused. For a guy who typically makes such fast decisions, I sure am struggling with this one."

If you're faced with this problem, there's probably a part of you that feels guilty even complaining about all the opportunity. That's what my clients are telling me anyway. Many of us were taught to be grateful for what we have, and you certainly remember a time when things weren't so great. How can you complain when things are so good? The truth is you complain because you're exhausted from the work, from the overload of good ideas. You complain because all these opportunities are forcing you to make some tough choices. If only you had two choices, you tell yourself, then your decision would be easy. When you have too many options, it's frustrating because you have to make the right decision among a field of possibilities.

Please stop beating yourself up for being frustrated. You have to know it's perfectly okay to be looking for a solution to your challenge.

The answer: Accept the fact that you deserve all this success.

You're probably afraid if you say no to an opportunity, you'll lose it forever. Maybe you even remember the times when you would kill for the experience. And here you are: full of more opportunities than you ever dreamed. Trust that if you're attracting such titillating opportunities. You will always attract amazing things. You will.

Along the way, you will have to let some alluring things go. That's the way it is. You can always change your Power of Three focus areas next week if something better comes long. But for right now, it's time to decide on your top three focus areas.

3. **You don't know what to do with everything else you're expected to accomplish.**

The very first thing that pops into most people's heads when doing this Power of Three exercise is what you're going to do with everything else. If the goal is to spend 80 percent of your time on the things that matter, what do you do with everything else? Great question. Keep reading for the answers.

THE POWER OF NO

Here's what happens when people decide they want to get more balance in their lives. They try to add in a whole bunch of new stuff right away: a new exercise program, coaching the kid's soccer team, going back to church and signing up to be on a committee, set weekly dates with their spouse, schedule weekly get-togethers with their friends, etc. Yikes. There is a time for everything, but not a time to do everything. And what you're trying to do at the office is everything.

Rich, the client I told you about earlier, said it best:

Connecting work and tasks to the bottom line is simply the most important skill needed in the fast-paced, competitive business environment, but it is often the least understood. Helping my team understand what we weren't going to do was really more important than helping them understand what they were going to do.

Unless you figure out a way to help your people stayed focused on those activities that drive the bottom line, you will not achieve the results you want. There are too many things enticing them to run in another direction, many exciting things popping up to pull their attention off what you want.

Once you've helped them identify what areas are most important – their Power of Three – then it's time to determine what goes off the plate. The rule of thumb is anything that doesn't relate to the Power of Three gets trashed. Yes, everything. I know, you hate to let things go. Most of us do, but it's vitally important to achieving the outcomes you want.

Action step

Go back to the lists that your team brought to your meeting and take a look at the activities that don't fall into your Power of Three. What things do you need to eliminate immediately? These are tough choices, I understand that. Give your people – and yourself – the permission to trash 20 percent of what's on your plates right now. What is going to go?

Then develop an action plan to let these things go gracefully. If they impact other people, be sure to create a strategy so you honor the relationships. Telling the truth is often the best advice in these cases. Most people will understand your reasoning if you take the time to confess what's truly going on.

YOUR RESISTANCE

Let's talk about your resistance to saying no to some key things on the plate. Here's what most leaders tell me immediately shows up as a block to letting projects and activities go.

1. **You don't believe there is a way to take stuff off the plate, so you don't want to open that can of worms.**

This one always makes me laugh because burying your head in the sand has never been the answer to anything. We need leaders in our organizations who are able to make the tough calls. We desperately need people who are willing to stand strong amidst the adversity. Avoiding the issue is not the answer, and you know that.

2. You don't want to let anyone down, and you know you will.

Whenever my clients use this excuse, I always say: "Is that person's life more important than your own?" Fundamentally, when you put someone else's needs before your own, that's exactly what you're doing. You're saying their issues, needs or concerns are more important than yours. Are they? I didn't think so.

The cycle has to stop somewhere, and I want it to stop with you right here, right now. Any time you say no to a project and have to endure the pain of letting someone down, you will think much more carefully in the future before you agree to take something on. See how powerful the Power of Three is? It allows you to say yes to the things that matter and no to the things that you truly don't have energy or capacity to handle *before* they become an issue. You're really the one who got yourself in this situation by saying you would take on an assignment when it had nothing to do with your 90-day goals.

So take a deep breath and do what you have to do.

3. **You're going to look bad if you pull the plug on a project you committed to completing.**

The only response I have to this is how bad are you going to look if your team doesn't do their best work? That's exactly what will happen if you're taking on work that has nothing to do with driving company goals. The reality is you're overloaded and don't have the capacity to do more work than the activities that truly matter to your goals. Your team is in the same boat. Instead, by saying yes to these new things, everyone is going to have to rush to get the not-so-important assignments completed. The outcome: the team will do a good job rather than a great job.

Trust me. You'll look worse if you show up with mediocre work. Design your workload so you and the team can be exceptional every time. Yes, every time. Keep saying no to anything and everything that doesn't fit into your Power of Three.

4. **It's not acceptable in your environment if you don't do certain things.**

Okay, so I'll give you this one. There are some things that you have to do like fill out expense reports, attend company meetings, sort through email, go through your mail . . . the list goes on. The reality is most people let this administrative stuff eat up their time, and they never give momentum the ability to kick in. The Power of Theme Days solves this problem.

THE POWER OF THEME DAYS

The thing I know to be true is no matter how disciplined and focused you are, if the people around you aren't that way, you're going to be pulled into their situations and crises. How many times have you sat down to plan your day, and when you showed up at the office, someone else had a different idea for you? Yes, a lot. The Power of Theme Days eliminates this problem.

Here's how they work. At the beginning of the month (or the year), you sit down and identify what theme you're going to give each day. When I use the word theme, I'm referring to the activity you're committing to spending the entire day working on. Can you imagine spending an entire day on revenue-producing activities or an entire day only on administrative stuff? Yes, you'd get a lot done if you could give yourself a full day of concentration on a particular area.

That's exactly what Theme Days are. A day where you'll be spending a huge chunk of concentrated time focused. Most of our clients identify their Theme Days as Laser Days, Support Days and Free Days.

On Laser Days, they spend the day working on revenue-producing activities. No meetings, no going through the mail, no "can I talk to you for just a minute" conversations. They invest their time on their Power of Three areas and nothing else.

On Support Days, they spend the day working on administrative stuff, the work they generated during their Laser Days. These are the days they sort through email, return phone calls, attend staff meetings, anything that supports their Power of Three activities.

On Free Days, they take the entire day off. No voicemails, no planning, not one minute of work on a Free Day.

But don't think you have to use Laser, Support and Free as your themes. We've had clients build in Creative Days for idea generation, Staff Days for team-building activities, Recruiting Days for interviewing candidates, Planning Days for long-range planning, and Political Days for navigating through the political environment at their companies. Anything that's important to you that demands concentrated time to get the right results needs it's own Theme Day. The trick is to sit down with your calendar and schedule these things in. Right away.

Action step

The first step in using the Power of Theme Days is deciding what themes you need your days to take. What areas in your work need concentrated attention? Make a list of the type of days you'd like to have.

The second step is to identify how many days you need to support this theme. Perhaps you need three Laser Days a week right now because you're trying to reach a high goal. Maybe you're so buried in administrative crap that you need three Support Days a week. I'm sure you need some Planning Days as most leaders blow these important activities off because they aren't urgent and staring them in the face. Decide how many of each day you need.

The third step is to start marking out the time in your

calendar. When I used a paper calendar, I loved to use color highlighters to indicate what theme day it was. Yellow was for Laser Days, green was for Support Days and pink was for Free Days. Obviously, if you use a Palm Pilot, you can't use colored markers. Take the time to give each day a theme.

The fourth and final step is to actually follow your plan. If you don't, you'll never access the Power of Theme Days.

GET YOUR PEOPLE ON BOARD

Whenever we introduce this concept to our clients, they immediately fall in love with it. They understand how much more they'd get done if they would give themselves chunks of time to concentrate and do great work. But when they start to implement the idea, they find that unless other people on their teams are doing the same thing, it takes an incredible amount of energy to fend other people off.

You must get your entire team to build their schedules around Theme Days. Imagine how many results would be accomplished if everyone spent two full days on revenue-producing activities. Ah, now you get the power of this!

Every single organization that uses this philosophy sees huge results from it. Brian and his team of fifteen salespeople certainly did. I started coaching Brian four years ago because he was faced with a challenge most managers today deal with. Not only was Brian the sales manager, but he was also expected to produce revenue himself. When I first started working with him, Brian spent almost 80 percent of his time on his own customers and very little time with his sales reps. His team was floundering, but every month they made their overall numbers. Why? Brian was generating 70 percent of the team's goals.

Once I determined that Brian truly did want to be the manager of his team, we could get to work on achieving results in both responsibility areas. Sometimes when I see this type of thing happening – the manager more interested in producing his or her own results than inspiring the team – it makes me believe that person wants to be the top producer, not the leader. In Brian's case, he simply didn't know how to be successful at both.

The first thing we did was identify the Power of Three areas for both his management role and his sales role. He ended up with five focus areas: two for his managerial role (People and Politics) and three for his sales role (Prospecting, Presenting and Closing). Next, we implemented the Power of Theme Days to allow Brian the ability to get the most important things done. Mondays were his Manager Days where he spent the entire day working with his team, handling internal issues, whatever he needed to do to be the boss. Tuesdays and Wednesdays became his Sales Days where he focused his attention on meeting with clients and closing deals. Thursdays became his Support Days where he handled the administrative parts that went along with doing deals, and Fridays were another Manager Day.

Once Brian had his Theme Day schedule down, he communicated his game plan with his team, and he got them on board following a similar system. When they were all working on support activities on the same day, the typical complaints that Brian wasn't available went away. Momentum kicked into gear as the team became a well-oiled machine with everyone focused on the same thing at the same time. Conflicts decreased, the work was getting done, and sales went through the roof. Brian went from generating 70 percent of the total team revenue to less than 20 percent while his personal sales numbers went up by 25 percent. His people starting getting the sales simply because they harnessed the power of momentum.

Action step

Once you've identified your Theme Days, pull your team together and have them do the same thing. Then schedule Theme Days for the entire department. Be sure that everyone has the same Theme Day on the same day. All Laser Days need to be the same days of the week, Support Days on the same days. If people are doing their own Theme Day schedules without rolling those into what the rest of the team wants, you'll experience conflict. For example, you'll want to schedule a staff meeting on your Support Day but during someone else's Laser Day. Get everyone in sync with the master schedule. It'll drive them wild to accomplish more every day than they have in a long time.

SIMPLICITY IS THE KEY

In an overly complex world, simplicity is the key. If you want to achieve the right results, laser focus is crucial. If you want to retain your people, give them the ability to accomplish something that matters. And that requires laser focus. If you want to get people home at a decent hour without sacrificing results, laser focus is the only way you'll do it.

The lesson?

> **Great leaders spend their time focusing on what matters. They help their people focus on what matters. And the rest goes in the trash can.**

IT DRIVES THEM CRAZY WHEN . . .

1. You think the problems would go away if they only learned how to better manage their time.
2. You keep piling things on the plate without taking assignments away.
3. They are distracted by too many ideas and opportunities.
4. No one helps them prioritize what truly matters.
5. They spend the day doing work, but don't feel as if they accomplished anything.
6. Any idea is a good idea, and it goes on the To-Do list. No one has the capacity to say no.
7. You aren't able to choose between a wide variety of opportunities. You direct the team to try them all.
8. You won't pull the plug on a project that clearly isn't important.
9. You go from one thing to another all day long. And you expect your people to do the same thing.

10. You love to complicate things. Who's heard of K-I-S-S (Keep it simple, stupid)?

IT DRIVES THEM WILD WHEN . . .

1. You know what activities drive the bottom line. And you focus their work in that direction.
2. You help them trash what doesn't matter.
3. You lead the charge of helping your team prioritize and only put your attention to the top three focus areas.
4. You understand the power of momentum – and you use it.
5. You know how to say no. In a good way.
6. You easily pull the plug on projects that are clearly not adding impact to team results.
7. You fight distraction all day long. And they love it when you fight for them.
8. You pride yourself on being reasonable on how much can get done in any given day.
9. You love using Theme Days because then everyone is on the same page.
10. Simplicity is your middle name.

Use speed to your advantage

This is the world of the Internet. We walk fast, talk fast, eat fast and then say, "I gotta run." Most people are either jazzed by our sped-up world or they're exhausted by its intensity.

O N ONE HAND, you know you have to move fast in order to stay ahead of your competition. Your customers expect immediate response to requests, and you yourself hate to wait in lines. Instant gratification is the name of the game. Most consultants preach that in business today, speed is the imperative. I agree with them.

But I'm not for speed for speed's sake. You need to take time to make major decisions and to rest when you're tired. If you don't, you know you'll end up running yourself into the ground. I'm not for speed for speed's sake. Leaders today need a new way to achieve speed with direction and accuracy.

What's the point of going fast if you don't get the results you want? You'll burn your people out, and they won't have the capacity to keep running at such an intense pace.

As Ron Mudge, one of the coaches on our team, recently said, "Watching the scenery when you're going 55 m.p.h. gives you a much different view than if you're riding a bike or walking down the road. Different speeds give you different perspectives." Well said.

The problem is most people run around putting out fires without paying attention to what they're doing. All they do is see life from their perspective in the fast lane, and it's frankly not enough. What would they see if they slowed down to the speed of riding a bike? What are they missing because they're not walking the course?

In order to succeed today, it's vital that you get your arms around this issue. There are times to go fast, and there are times to go slow. There are times to rely on technology, and there are times to rely on human capital.

Unless you figure out what's the right speed for different situations, you and your team will end up dead on the side of the road. And no one wants that.

DECIDE WHAT PACE IS RIGHT

Step 1: perform the right activities
The best way to gain back control in a sped-up world is to make sure you're doing the important tasks. If you want to use speed

as a competitive advantage, then by all means make sure you're doing the right things fast.

What often happens is you spend so much of your time running from here to there that you don't take time to ask yourself what truly matters. The faster you go, the narrower your focus must be. What if 80 percent of what you do in a single day adds no value at all? Ugh. Not the way to succeed in a fast-paced world.

So take a deep breath and ask yourself, "Does this matter?" If it does, great. If not, you have some changes to make. (If you don't know the answer to this question, you'll want to go back to Chapter #3: Maximize Productivity to determine what your most important focus areas are.)

Step 2: keep your eye on the long-term goal.

The best analogy I can use is that of a race car driver. Did you know that the No. 1 reason drivers crash at high speeds is because they focused on what was right in front of them? To travel at high speeds without crashing demands that you look beyond the turn. Drivers will tell you that the car is going too fast to maneuver quickly, and you need to look at what's coming rather than what's sitting in front of you. The second you put your attention on the turn, you crash right into it.

If you want to gain speed in your company, you need to look beyond what's on the plate today and look at what's coming. Have you decided what will be here six months from now? When speed is your competitive advantage, someone on the team has to be constantly preparing for the next turn in the great race of business. As the leader, guess who's job that is?

Action step

If you haven't already determined what's next with your team and your business, now's the time. Grab your calendar and schedule an entire day away from the office to decide what the future looks like. What's on the horizon that you need to prepare for? Get it in writing and use that vision with your team.

Please ask your people to join you is they have the capacity to see the future. If they don't, find a group who can help you or hire an executive coach who specializes in vision work. It's vital you know what's next so you can do what's necessary to get there without crashing and burning.

Step 3: determine what's the best speed for each activity

I'm not foolish enough to believe that we have time to do everything at a slow, careful speed. We don't. The market demands that we move fast, that we are nimble, flexible and ever changing.

But faster is not always better. Do you want your eye surgeon to be faster or better? I think most of us would go for the best and most methodical work when dealing with our eyes.

What's also true is you cannot sacrifice talent for speed. There have been times in my business when I hired someone because we desperately needed them to get the work done. Every time – and I mean every time – we didn't take the time to find the ideal person to fill that role, these new hires turned out to be complete disasters. Hiring too quickly and taking people on because there's too much to do is a bad move. Always a bad move.

Think carefully about the right speed to do a particular activity. Maybe what the situation calls for is a twenty-four-hour delay. Or no activity at all. Most leaders don't take the time to decide what activities require speed and which ones don't. You're too caught up in trying to move things off the To-Do list to the Done list. It drives your people crazy when all they do is rush around.

Action step

One of the best ways to look at the speed issue is to have each person on your team make a master list of the activities they need to accomplish in any given month. This includes returning voicemail messages, major and minor projects, anything they invest time doing. (You have probably already completed this task if you stepped in to do any of the other Action Steps I've recommended in this book.)

Next to each activity, decide what the appropriate turnaround time is to complete that task. For example, at my company we have a standard that email is responded to in twenty-four hours even if it's as simple as "We got your message. Thank you. We need to take another day to find the answer to your question." My pet peeve is when I send an email, and I don't get a response for days. Once you create the standards for the major chunks of work, you can work on a daily basis to speed up the process or slow it down based on circumstances that pop up.

What's great about this exercise is your team will start to become very clear on what activities demand speed and those that require more time. There's often a disconnect between what the leader believes is appropriate turn-around times and what the employees think. This action step will open up that conversation.

Step 4: build the infrastructure to support fast-paced work

If your business demands that you move at high speeds, then make sure your systems are set up to handle the intensity. Cars made in Germany are designed to travel at speeds of 100 m.p.h., and highways there are built to support that speed. In the US, when we try to travel that fast, our cars break down or the highways are too dangerous for a safe journey. No, not because we can't go that fast. We can. Our transportation systems simply aren't designed to go at such intense speeds. Infrastructure matters when you want to go faster.

If market conditions demand fast-paced work, make sure you have the systems in place to support the speed. If not, you'll end up breaking down or getting in a terrible wreck. This is not the time to drive an American-made car on the Autobahn.

One of my clients, Michelle, faced this very dilemma. When we first started working together, Michelle hired me to help her develop a three-year strategic plan for her business unit. She's the vice president of a Internet company that's already gone public, and Michelle was struggling with the 'what's next?' question. Her team's entire focus had been on taking the company public, and when she decided to stay with the organization after the IPO, Michelle knew she needed a new vision.

As we dived in to examine the various directions she could take her division, it became crystal clear that Michelle and her team had an unique opportunity that no one else seemed to be targeting. The secret would be to get into that market fast and dominate while the rest of her competitors were asleep. Her initial reaction was to immediately jump in and design the go-to-market plan as they went along. Her knee-jerk reaction was to go fast after this target market.

I didn't support that idea. Michelle needed some time to make sure her team had everything they needed to succeed at this new strategy. No, I don't mean that I wanted her to take weeks to put everything in place. I wanted her to be sure her team could handle the intensity this new market would require. Remember, they had just come off an IPO, and Michelle would burn her folks out if she moved faster than her people were capable of going.

How many times have you asked your people to perform with less than what they needed to do the job? And then you turn around and do the same thing again and again? That's not the way to inspire your team and get the results you want.

Michelle, her three directors and I spent eight hours the next day putting together their plan. This included identifying every resource her team needed to succeed. If they had to go to market right away, what systems, processes and resources did they need to put in place? We then created an action plan with specific timelines to build the infrastructure. Michelle took the responsibility of getting the rest of the organization to shift their priorities in support of this new strategy. Her managers took on the load of getting the right equipment, people, training and accountabilities to champion this effort.

That one day of planning made all the difference.

The result? They made a huge impact on an untapped market without burning through their people or their resources. Simply because they thought ahead on what this strike fast approach needed to succeed.

Action step

What resources and support structures do you need to have in place that prevents breakdowns? Brainstorm with your team about what they need to operate at a fast pace. Then invest time and money getting these items in place. You may need to upgrade your phone system, install high-speed Internet connections, buy new computers or hire more administrative support. And you made need to add major enhancements to what you're doing before you can rev up. My point: Get the resources list developed so you can start executing against it. And then make these things happen.

Step 5: know when to rest

Jogging can teach you a lot about business.

I remember when I decided I wanted to become a jogger. I've never been much of a runner. I never ran track in high school, never played any sports where you had to train by running sprints or taking a few laps around the track. I did aerobics or took dance classes instead, but I was always envious of people who called themselves joggers.

For a long time, I wanted to live the fantasy I had in my head. I wanted to start my day by running five miles. I wanted the clarity that comes from intense exercise. I wanted to be like all those people I knew who ran.

I made the classic error of thinking I was in shape to start a full-fledge jogging program because I started walking regularly a few years earlier. Let me tell you, it's not the same.

The day arrived when I was going to start my new running program. I laced up my shoes, did a few stretches and went out the front door. I had decided that morning that I'd walk a few blocks to get myself warmed up, but I was itching to get started. So I started running.

For the first block or so, I imagined I was running a marathon. I mean, why start a running program if you're not going to go for the gusto? The wind was blowing through my hair, and I was loving it. But I didn't have a plan, and I didn't have a partner to keep me going. I just thought I'd run until my body gave out.

I was exhausted by block three. Right then, one of my neighbors drove by, honked the horn and waved. That kept me going for another block when I had to stop and walk. I looked at my watch. It turns out I ran for a total of five minutes!

This running is a lot harder than it looks. And it's a great analogy for business. Are you trying to run a marathon as if it were a three-mile race? Many leaders I know focus too much on the short-term and forget the race is won by those who stay in the game. Yet at the same time, many leaders focus too much on the long-term and forget about the quarterly numbers. Again, a disaster.

The No. 1 lesson I learned when I started running: Know when to rest. That first week of jogging was one of the most gruelling experiences for me. I had set this goal to run every day for a month, and for the first week, that's exactly what I did. For anyone who runs regularly, you know this is the fastest way to injury. By day seven, I had actually lost ground because my body couldn't keep up the pace. I took a few days off to recover, and I was able to run for fifteen minutes the next time I went out. That recovery period is vital if you want to win the race.

When you don't allow your team to rest, to replenish and renew, you're doing the same thing I did to my body when I started running. You're forcing them to lose ground. How many times have you asked your people to turn on the heat to reach a huge goal and then as soon as they reach it, you ask them to do it again? No one can function this way week after week. You must allow your people to take time off when it's time to rest. If you don't, you'll have problems. Guaranteed.

Action step

If you're in the midst of pushing your team right now to achieve something big, be sure to give them time to recover when they reach the goal. This is an absolute must. Yes, even if you have to put off starting something else that's important for a week or two.

Your people need the time to recover or you won't get top performance from them on the next project. Eventually, their bodies and spirits will give out on them – and you'll end up with mediocrity. Or worse, they'll leave the company. That's not the risk a leader can afford to take.

Step 6: give your team time to improve

The second lesson I learned when I started running: It takes time to succeed. Everything we do in business is a process, and it takes time to accomplish your goals. When you're focused on succeeding – whether it be in doubling your sales or being a strong leader or growing a profitable business – it takes time. You can't start running one day and think you can run a marathon the next. You have to work up to it.

That means every day you need to focus on the small steps your team can take. What action can you and your team take today that will get you one step closer to your goal? Good. Then do that. It's much too easy to pay attention to what everyone else is doing and get caught up in comparing yourself to them. Running the race has to do with harnessing the collective power of your team, not spending your time focused on the competition.

I understand there's a part of you that doesn't have the

patience to wade through the learning curve. You have a choice: fire your entire team and replace it with people who know exactly what they're doing and can deliver results in twenty-four hours. Too extreme? That's exactly what you do to your people when you keep driving them to move beyond the learning curve. You drive them crazy when you don't give them room to improve their skills.

ACTING LIKE A GREAT LEADER

One of the reasons we've become obsessed with speed is because our world has gone technocrazy. Everywhere you turn, you're hearing about the new and improved technologies impacting every facet of our lives. DNA researchers tell you decoding the human genome will allow you to perfect the human species. Web mavericks share with you a dream of how you'll be able to do 100 percent of your shopping and communicate with the world sitting in your pajamas. And we get caught up in their visions.

These products are coming to market incredibly fast, and that speed creeps its way into your world. You find yourself wanting everything done faster and faster. You don't want to wait for reports. You expect your people to turn major projects around in two days or less, and you get impatient when they ask for more time. You start getting anxious because things aren't moving fast enough, and you begin doubting your team's ability to get the job done.

It has nothing to do with speed. It has everything to do with your expectations. You must learn how to take back control, to stand tall no matter how many new technologies are hitting the market. Are you using speed as a competitive advantage or as yet another way to be dissatisfied?

Now I do not advocate that you run to the woods to escape the technocraziness. I'm not going to suggest that you simplify your life and bury your head in the sand. Not at all. The greatest part of all the technological advances is they create tremendous change in our lives. And change is good. No matter how many times your head is spinning, all this technocraziness is good for you as long as you put things in perspective. Did you get that? The way to succeed in today's economy is to know when technology improves performance and when it just adds to the crap on your desk.

Here are two ideas on how to take back control in a sped-up world.

1. Stop being a firefighter.

One of the reasons you feel as if you're pulled in a hundred directions every day is you spend too much time band aiding problems rather than solving them forever. It's that short-term vs. long-term problem.

When I was doing research for this book, a bunch of my clients told me their biggest problem was not having enough time to focus on the big picture. "I spend my entire day handling crisis and issues, Jen," Joe said one morning in the middle of a coaching session. "It's no wonder we don't get the big results I know my team can achieve. I feel like a firefighter rushing to save the house."

One of the challenges of our accelerated workplace is many people walk around with the words "Fire! Fire!" in their heads. They race from problem to another to save the day. Yet many leaders fail at solving the problem. They come up with short-term solutions with the belief that when things slow down then the permanent solution will find its way into the mix. Things never slow down, and a vicious cycle begins.

To be a great leader today, you must find the source of the problem and handle that. No more band aids. No more quick fixes. It may seem as if you're taking care of a lot of issues, but what you're really doing is avoiding the inevitable.

One of our clients, Michael, was one of the best firefighters I know. As the CEO of a fast-growing manufacturing firm, Michael knew how to handle any crisis that showed up at his front door. He would put off one vendor in order to pay another when cash flow was tight. When the second vendor would call to complain, he'd do the same thing with another supplier. Michael would take weak managers and move them to another department in the hopes their performance would improve. He rarely fired anyone; he simply shifted their job responsibilities. When a customer called with a complaint, Michael was there to do whatever the customer wanted no matter what the request. And many times those requests caused major problems somewhere else.

What I got Michael to see was how high a price he was paying by not solving problems with permanent solutions. He needed to get funding in place so he didn't have to run his accounts payable department in a constant state of crisis. Michael needed to overhaul his management team to support the new growth the company was experiencing. And he needed to make sure that customer requests could be easily fulfilled without disrupting other customers' delivery dates.

Firefighting got him into trouble. Developing long-term solutions saved his business.

Action step

One of the best ways to shift out of firefighter mode is to start tracking the fires you're putting out all day long. Every single time you're called in to solve a problem, make a note in your Palm Pilot or planner. At the end of the week, look at what problems keep showing up again and again. Is there one employee involved in each of these situations? You have a performance issue with that person. Once you handle their performance deficits, the problems will go away. Is your computer system constantly crashing? Upgrade your system, and the problems go away. Is one customer calling in and they're never satisfied? Let that customer go, and the problems go away.

Your focus is to search for the source of the problem, and then handle that. You fix the problem forever when you go to the source.

2. Don't let technology replace the human touch.

Have you ever sent an email that was misinterpreted? Ah, come on. I know you have. You type out an email in two minutes or less, and the next thing you know, your entire employee base is in an uproar. They misinterpreted what you had written, and the entire thing was blown out of proportion. Right when you thought you could solve a problem in less than two minutes by sending an email, you end up having to spend three days calming your people down.

One of the major problems with these major improvements in communications is people believe technology can build relationships. It can't. More and more, leaders are hiding behind computer screens and voicemail messages, using the excuse that they're too busy to meet in person any more.

I understand you're busy, but if you want to gain back control in a rapid world, you need to get out of your cave and spend time with your people. That's the single best way to build loyalty and retain your people. Email and voicemail is great for supporting a relationship and keeping in touch. Your people still need your human touch.

Don't have time? Ugh. You need to make room for this. Your people are the reason you're the leader, and the only way to fight against so much intensity is to be present with them. Your time with them makes all the difference.

Action plan

Building relationships takes time. You know that, so what are you doing to build powerful relationships with your team? Create an action plan right now to spend more time with the talent in your organization. It could be a monthly lunch with a few key people or quarterly business trips to meet with customers. The point isn't what you do, it's that you do it. Develop a plan to meet in real time with your team. And follow through with your ideas. Hiding behind technology isn't the answer. Being with them is.

USE SPEED WITH YOUR EMPLOYEES

It's one thing to think about using speed with your customers or increasing the speed in which you impact a new market. It's quite another to use this same standard with your team.

Why is it that some leaders bust their butts to serve customers in twenty-four hours or less, but wait weeks to handle employee issues? I think it's because you start to take your people for granted. Don't do it. Every time you put off your people and avoid handling a problem for them, you send the message that they aren't as important as everything else. If you're going to use speed as your competitive advantage, use this philosophy with your people.

Here are a few ways we've helped clients use speed with their teams to get great results.

1. Don't let civility and respect escape your life.

Yes, that means you return all voicemail and email you receive even if they're from employees you don't want to talk to. Why? Because you're being disrespectful every time you blow someone off.

I recently wanted to order something on the Internet from a

well-known company, but I had a question before I submitted my credit card information. So I sent an email asking my brief question. What I got back was an autoresponder telling me someone would get back with me in twenty-four hours. It's been two weeks and still no response. I bought the product somewhere else.

It's easy to criticize customer service departments, but take this philosophy and bring it home. Are you treating your people the same way? Some questions to ask yourself:

- When someone on your team sends you an email, do you respond right away or does it take a few days to get back with them?
- Do you return phone calls within twenty-four hours to your employees?
- How long does it typically take to handle a problem one of your employees asked you to address?
- Is this an acceptable turnaround time when handling customer problems?
- Are there people on your team you avoid for whatever reason?

When my coaches are working with groups of employees, slow decision making is perhaps the No. 1 complaint they have about their leaders. Civility and respect has gone right out the door as the work world has increased in velocity.

Please don't use the excuse that you're too busy. You can use technology to your advantage to respond quickly to employees issues even if it's as simple as an email that says, "Hey,

John, I'm still working on that issue you brought to my attention. I'm having problem getting so-and-so to call me back." It will drive your people wild if you handle their problems fast.

The point is to be gracious, polite and treat everyone with respect. When you don't respond to other people, you are saying that who are you is not someone to be respected. People who are respected take the time to communicate back.

To avoid spending your entire work day chained to email or the phone, schedule blocks of time to respond to requests. We coach our clients to spend the first hour of every day replying to email, and one day a week handling more complicated issues (what we call Support Days from Chapter 3). The more concentrated time you can give this task, the more you'll get done in less time. Try it, it works.

If you're tired of this rude world we live in, then change has to start with you. It's amazing how many times people contact my office and are shocked when I call them back. What does that tell you about the world we live in?

Action step

Make a commitment to yourself that you will respond to everyone who contacts you within forty-eight hours. I'd tell you to go for a twenty-four-hour turnaround, but if you can accomplish a two-day response time, that's probably a huge leap for you. You can work your way up to a one-day response time once you make the first tier. Do not hide behind your excuse that you're too busy. Call your people back. Email them quickly. Be willing to sort through their issues and give them the time they need. That's what leaders do.

2. Develop a fast feedback loop with your people.

One of the best things about the Internet is how fast you can get information from your customers. You can launch a new service at 8 a.m. and have tremendous feedback from hundreds of your customers by dinner time. The next morning, the service is tweaked to better serve your people. That's what I call using speed as your competitive advantage. It's getting the information you need and acting on it. Fast.

Great leaders today apply this same idea to their people. To compete in an accelerated marketplace, your employees need to know what's going on. Not tomorrow, but today. Just as importantly, you need to know what's going on with them so you can handle their issues with lightning speed. It's the waiting around for answers that causes the rumor mill to start flying.

One of my clients had a great idea on how to get information to his team fast, and he took the idea from Hollywood. If you've spent much time on the web reviewing the music industry, you'll notice that most of the popular artists have their own sites. They're designed and supported by the record companies to keep information current.

When a rumor starts circulating about a musician, their fans know to immediately go to the web to get the correct information. On these sites, the artists or publicists will tell the real truth about whatever that rumor is. "Yes, the rumor is true. Britney Spears was in Mall of America yesterday." Or "No, it's a ridiculous story, and she was never there."

This is a great way for artists to tell their side of the story without having to spend thousands of dollars releasing press releases. It's instanteous, and it works.

So Scott and I were having lunch talking about the incredible rumor mill at his company. He was complaining about how his entire day could be spent telling his side to the story when this idea suddenly popped into his head. What if he created a special area on their intranet that would do the same thing the record companies have done?

Every time he got wind of some story that was circulating among his team, he could go to the intranet and type out the truth. With a bit of training, his people would visit this area to get the real story, and rumors would be crushed almost as soon as they started.

I know, not much fun for the gossips out there, but what a great way to use speed to keep your team informed. That's what I call a fast response.

Action step

What can you do to develop a fast feedback loop with your people? When they need answers, they want them right away. Not tomorrow and not the next day. What steps can you take to speed up the way information is sent out to your team? Implement one new idea this week and see what results it brings.

A PERSONAL LESSON TO LEARN ABOUT SPEED

"What a waste of time! I hate it when people waste my time."

One of my clients said this to me recently, and I have to admit, I started laughing. No, I wasn't making fun of her. I was amused that many of my clients say the same thing.

What does that mean anyway? A big waste of time?

It seems your quest to be an effective time manager, to be extremely productive, has ripped the joy right out of your life. You're impatient when someone pops in your office for a morning chat. You have to work, you're thinking, and you end up ignoring what the person is saying because you're caught up in having to waste your time.

You're impatient in the line at the bank because you have more important things to do than hanging out waiting. You're crabby by the time you're done with your business there because you had to wait. You tap your toes while your employees are sharing an issue with you because you have a meeting to attend to. You're busy, going fast, and you have things to do. Anything that makes you slow down is, in your mind, a waste of time.

The irony is by focusing on the things you believe are wasting your time, you actually miss out on

some crucial opportunities. The best things are passing you by, but you're too wrapped up in yourself that you don't even see them. That's what makes me laugh.

Let me show you how you could change your focus from wasting your time to appreciating what's there. That person who's in your office "wasting your time" with their stories may actually be saying something that could spark a huge revenue-producing project for you. No, not because they know what they're saying, but because their words light a fire in one of your ideas.

This happened to me a few years ago. I was sitting in a convention hall bored out of my mind, feeling as if I was wasting my time, when this dull speaker asked an interesting question. The answer to that question launched a new coaching philosophy I developed which ended up being a huge profit center. We've quadrupled in size because I was able to shift out of feeling I wasting my time and instead I heard what that speaker had to say.

What if I had completely tuned out this woman? That revenue stream would not exist. Even the dumbest things can turn out to be huge revelations.

Let's go back to that line that you're so annoyed to be standing in. What if the person standing in front of you or behind you is that customer you've been dying to meet but he won't return your calls? You never know who's around you when you're too focused on rushing to the next thing on your schedule.

Please don't misunderstand. I'm not suggesting that you jam your schedule with administrative, valueless activities. To find value in everything you do – slow or fast – you need to stop spending so much time focused on the time you're "wasting," and learn to enjoy where you are.

What causes you to be impatient is often a mirror of what's happening in your own life. You will continue to experience these so-called wastes of time until you change. Instead of being annoyed while you wait, ask yourself, "Why am I so frustrated with this?" Perhaps your answer is the bank doesn't have enough help to handle their customers. That's a sign that somewhere in your life you haven't built up the right systems to support your customers. Maybe it's time to hire that assistant you've been putting off. The most simple things can have such a huge impact but only if you're paying attention.

The next time you find yourself saying, "This is a big fat waste of time," I want you to laugh. Then look for the insight you're supposed to see. Life has this great way of teaching you everything you need to know. It's up to you to pay attention and stop letting your obsession with speed force you to miss what life has to offer.

Only then will you understand what using speed to your advantage truly means.

IT DRIVES THEM CRAZY WHEN . . .

1. You push and push without giving them a break.
2. You tell them everything is important, and it had to be done yesterday.

3.   You don't give them the necessary resources they need to be successful.

4.   The intensity never stops. You expect them to be the Energizer bunnies and keep going and going and . . .

5.   You think your job is to be the firefighter so that's what you do all day long.

6.   You don't build the system to support high speeds. Equipment, systems and processes break and are put back together without permanent solutions.

7.   You hide behind technology because it's faster to communicate that way.

8.   There's only one speed in the company: fast.

9.   You don't take the time to decide what activities need to be done today and which ones need more time to do right.

10. You're impatient. And it shows.

IT DRIVES THEM WILD WHEN . . .

1.   You push them hard then give them a chance to catch their breath.

2.   You prioritize what's important and what can wait to be done.

3.   You give them everything they need to be brilliant on the job.

4.   You pace projects so they don't burn out.

5.   You hate being a firefighter. When a problem shows up, you go to the source and solve it. For good.

6.   You build the system to support intense work.

7.   You know when to use technology – and when to meet in person.

8.   You understand different speeds give you different per-

spectives. And you see the world from different vantage points.

9.   You constantly help them prioritize. And they love that about you.

10. You're impatient. But you look at what lesson you have to learn when your impatience kicks in. And you learn the lesson.

CHAPTER 5

Leverage strengths

As a leader, you probably spend way too much time focusing on the things that aren't working. That's a big problem for your people, but an even bigger problem for you.

THINK BACK TO the last few performance evaluations you've done with your team. If they're like most of the ones I hear about – or have had in my own career – they probably went something like this.

It's performance review time again. You've procrastinated for the last few weeks because you hate them just as much as your people do. In fact, when you mentioned that it was time for reviews, half your team turned up their noses. They want the salary increase without the review, and you can't blame them. Yet you know this is something that has to be done, something Human Resources thinks is good for your people, so you schedule time to prepare. It's for your staff, you tell yourself, and you do your best to get yourself ready for this important meeting.

You schedule an hour for each review, and for the first ten minutes or so, you and your employee are both feeling really good. You've spent the time highlighting the successes your employee has had during the year. You have even emphasized what a vital part they play on the team.

But you scheduled an hour for this review, so you immediately launch into what most companies called "opportunity areas." These are the areas where you want your employee to step up to a new level. You outline the behaviors and activities that will be a real stretch for them. Most of these, frankly, are not their strengths, but you want them to have a well-rounded career. It's time they overcame their weaknesses, you tell them during the review.

Perhaps you've decided to move them into a new role to see how fast they can overcome their not-so-strong skills. You remember a tough old manager who did the same to you, and look how your career turned out. You want similar success for your people, so you do the same thing that your old manager did to you.

When the review if over, what do your people do? The smart ones walk out of that meeting saying to themselves, "I really need to find a new job." And they follow through on that. Everyone else tells themselves they're ready to try something new, and they're willing to tackle these opportunity areas.

Most people will dive right in, putting their heart and souls into being something they're not. They stop focusing on what they're good at, and they invest time and attention on the things they're not so skilled at doing. That's what you told them to do, and they want to move up the ladder. So during the next twelve months, they make huge strides in the areas that needed the improvement. That's the great thing about your top talent. Anything they put their minds to, they will conquer.

Your disorganized employees get better at being organized. No, they're not a superstar at that skill, but they're better. Your introverts will become more outgoing – again, not the best, but pretty good. And your maverick let-me-do-it-myself people will become a little better at being part of the team.

When you sit down for the six-month or annual review, you acknowledge them for what they've accomplished. You marvel at the strides they've made in their opportunity areas, and like the last time, the cycle starts all over again with you setting the bar for your people to move outside their natural strength areas to focus on improving their weaknesses.

Did you ever step back to ask yourself if this "setting the bar so high" is driving them crazy?

In a few years, you have a team full of people with well-rounded skills. They're not the best at anything, but they're pretty good at a lot of things. The key areas where they could have become superstars – their strength areas – have been left alone while your people made improvements in weak areas. They ended up with exactly what you wanted: balanced in their skillsets.

But what you also have is a team that's not having much fun. Oh sure, they're getting the work done, but there isn't the intensity or the pizzazz you want your team to have. They pretty much look the same on paper, and you're starting to get concerned that they're not reaching new levels of success. They doing the same thing year after year, improving a little bit, but you're frustrated because you know they could do so much more.

Add to that challenge is you're not even sure who's going to take over your job when you move on. No one stands out in this crowd.

The truth is you did this to them. You crushed their ability to shine by having them to focus on those darn opportunity areas. You took their strengths, the skills they could have used to make a real impact, tossed them aside and had them focus their attention on getting better at their weaknesses. What you created was a dull group of people who look and act like everyone else.

A marketing consultant I know, Vickie Sullivan, said it best: "Anything that becomes abundant becomes diluted. And any-thing that is diluted becomes a commodity."

Yes, you got it. Your people became commodities because they focused on being like everyone else. No wonder you can't make real inroads on creativity or innovation with your team.

No wonder you can't get them to think for themselves or look at the numbers differently or do whatever it is you want them to do. You trained them to focus on their weaknesses and eliminate them. You trained them to disregard their strengths, what they could shine at doing, to put their attention in other areas. Now they're walking around wondering what impact their work is truly having on the company. They're asking themselves why they're always coming up a little bit short, why it is they know a lot of stuff but not not know much of anything. They're as confused as you are on what went wrong because they followed the rules and didn't end up with the result they wanted. They end up beating themselves up for not being good enough.

You need your people to be the best of the best, to be the Michael Jordan, Wayne Gretzky or Tiger Woods of your industry. In this highly competitive marketplace, you need them to be on the front of the curve, coming up with new ideas that become profitable solutions to business problems. In today's economy, hot ideas combined with solid execution is the key to unlocking tremendous success, but only the best of the best can pull this off.

If only we could get business success by having the right technology or the right processes. Almost every accomplishment comes down to how your people perform, and you've created a system that encourages them to be mediocre.

Your best people don't walk around wondering what impact their work is doing. They don't focus on the things they're not good at – they know what they shine at doing, and they seek out opportunities to get even better at the things they do well. When they light up, so does your bottom line.

The worse thing about putting so much attention on opportunity areas is many companies start doing the same thing in the marketplace. Rather than focusing on what they could shine at doing, they become "me, too" companies. Soon they're competing on price because when you're a commodity, that's what you do. and you know what happens when you start playing a price game. Your profits plummet, you become obsess with getting more market share in order to increase revenues, and you drive your people into the ground because they're rushing around trying to be everything to everyone.

Successful companies don't compete on price, they focus on what they do well and become even more masterful at that. You must take this same philosophy and apply it to your people. It's impossible not to feel as if you're making an impact when you're in the flow, doing the things you do naturally well and getting results from your efforts. That's the secret of success, you know. Putting yourself in the right situations where you can be brilliant.

It's your job as a leader to help your people leverage their strengths, what they're darn good at, in order to get the results you want. And yes, it's also your job to leverage the strengths of the company, do what you're darn good at, in order to get the results you want. My whole point is you have to come from a position of strength in the marketplace with your products and services – and especially with your people.

THE RETENTION SECRET

Here's another reason why you have to shift your mindset away from getting work done to leveraging from your people's strengths: if you don't, they're not going to stay. Maybe for the next few years they'll stick around and try it your way. But eventually they're going to say enough is enough. You have no idea how many clients work with my career coaches on this issue. Your people will start to feel depleted and bummed out with their careers. They can't see what they're great at, and they're constantly beating themselves up for not achieving more, for not making a real impact, for not doing work that matters. Eventually, they either shut themselves off emotionally and show up to do the bare minimum. Or worse, they seek out opportunities in other companies. They believe that the reason they're not shining must have something to do with their current position – or with you as the leader. Off they go to somewhere else.

When you're interested retaining your employees, the first place to look is at the things you do to drive your people away. No, not at how much money you're paying them – or not paying them – but at the way you show up as a leader. Remember, the Gallup Research Group tells us most employees leave for two reasons: (1) they don't like their manager or (2) they don't feel challenged or that they're making a contribution.

Shift your focus away from what isn't working to what is. Here's an example of how focusing on your strengths drives the right results and retains your key talent.

Andy hired my company to help develop his leaders. As a

fast-growing high-tech company, Andy needed his team to be able to produce results and do it fast. He knew his thirty-year-old managers were probably not as skilled with people as they needed to be, so Andy begged me to work with his team. The reason he had to resort to begging was his company was in a real mess. There were tremendous territorial issues going on between departments, and his managers' strong egos were getting in the way. I called it the Alpha Dog syndrome. Every one was fighting to be the top dog, and it was causing havoc in the organization. You can imagine what impact this fighting among the leaders was having on morale.

That's precisely the reason Andy hired us – his company was experiencing the beginning signs of substantial turnover. Andy personally sat down with each departing employee to find out why they were leaving. He discovered people were fed up with the infighting between his leaders. Andy knew his leaders had to change or the company wasn't going to make it.

The first thing I did was sit down with Andy and determine what he was personally brilliant at doing. What parts of being the CEO did he shine at? What areas did he shy away from? He got very clear that he was trying to be the CEO he thought he "should" be rather than the leader he was. That's a very important distinction. When you start to own your gifts, your natural talents, you begin to feel more comfortable with who you are. You start to shed the desire to be like everyone else, and you can begin to master what skills you already have.

That's exactly what Andy did. He immediately stopped trying to prove himself to his management team and his investors because he had clarity on the talents he was bringing to the job. As a thirty-five-year-old CEO, Andy had been caught up in acting like a middle-aged company president and not fully leveraging his youth, enthusiasm and quick mind.

Any time I see territorial issues going on in an company, I immediately go to the CEO to find out what's going on. Andy's own insecurities caused him to walk around with a chip on his shoulder, and his leadership team reflected that attitude. Never underestimate the impact your behavior has on your people.

But our coaching work had just begun. We then developed individual coaching relationships with Andy's six key leaders, and we worked with them to identify their strengths. Again, they were so focused on highlighting what others were doing wrong – and beating themselves up privately about not being good enough – these leaders weren't able to show up in a powerful way.

Two out of the six leaders decided their strengths had nothing to do with being a leader of people, and they both moved into more strategic, technically driven positions. It's important to know: those moves were their choices. When you become clear on who you are and what value you bring to the marketplace, you start to make choices based on where you want to spend your time. Leading people was too painful for these two managers. They both were smart enough to leverage their skillsets somewhere else.

Six months later, Simon was responsible for spinning off a new division for Andy's company, and he's having a ball creating something new. Once that division is up and running, Simon will be off starting something new. Developing and launching something new is what he shines at doing.

In 90 days, Andy saw a huge turnaround at his company. His managers discovered a new appreciation for the skills each person brought on the leadership team. They started asking their employees how they could help them leverage their strengths, and suddenly, retention was no longer an issue. Their people began to feel that despite the crazed work environment, they were working in areas that made a real difference.

WHAT ABOUT THE WORK?

So you're pushing back on this idea already? There are some of you who are saying to yourself, "But Jen, you don't understand what it's like to work at my company. I need my people to take on new responsibilities every day. We're growing so fast (or moving so fast or acquiring companies so fast – you fill in the blank) that we don't have time to focus on strengths. There's too much to get done. I don't see how this is going to work." At least you're being honest.

Most companies are moving at such an intense pace that the leaders don't take the time to identify who's the right person for the job. They give assignments to anyone who can can or will do the work, and they push the team to move even faster. I've been there before, let me tell you. Sometimes there is so much on my desk, I don't really care who does the work as long as it gets done. Yet every single time I turn away from

Brilliances

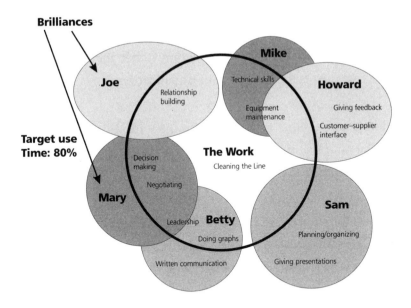

Target use Time: 80%

Figure 5.1 Redesign the work

asking myself, "Who's the right person for this job?" something goes wrong with the work. A client gets upset because my detail-oriented, task-driven assistant was abrupt to them. My other kinder, gentler assistant would have been much better at that assignment. On the flip side, when I ask my creative assistant to do detailed spreadsheets, it turns out to be not quite right whereas my other assistant would have done it perfectly. The work got done, but not at the level that I wanted.

I understand your cynicism to this idea. You're concerned if you let everyone only do what they're good at, there will be a huge amount of important work that will never get done. First, the goal for leveraging people strengths is to have them work in these areas 80 percent of the time. That leaves 20 percent for other "must do" activities. Second, you don't have to be at 80 percent right now. Let's gradually move into that target so it becomes a natural transition rather than something else that upsets the flow of your organization.

Here's an example of a client of mine who did this exercise. Notice that the majority of what needs to get done is covered by his people's strengths areas.

John is the director in a Fortune 100 company. He's been there for years and has worked his way up the corporate ladder. John is now responsible for eight direct reports who are working to change the way business is done at the company. He leads a small yet fierce team.

When John decided to leverage the strengths of his people, he too was concerned that the majority of work would fall through the cracks. Rather than roll out this idea to his employees, he and I worked on developing a plan first. If it didn't work out paper, John would have not have to deal with starting something new then pulling it away. We did this entire exercise behind closed doors to make sure it worked. It did.

Take a look at Figure 5.1 on page 163. You'll see that the circle in the middle reflects the scope of the work that needs to get done. Each corresponding circle indicates the strength areas for each of John's employees. Only a small percentage of work was left to be picked up by the team. What happened when John rolled this out throughout his team? You got it. Results went through the roof because each person worked from a position of strength rather than a position of weakness.

Remember, strength areas don't mean that your people have mastered that skillset. It means they have the capacity to be amazing because it ties in with who they are and what they're all about. The more they work in areas where they're gifted, the more talented they'll become over time.

If you want to move fast and create breakthrough results, you must harness the natural power of your team. Leveraging your people's strengths allows you to get the work done at a level you never experienced at a pace the market wants. Put a natural salesperson in a sales role and voilà! More sales. Put an introvert who's obsessed with the details in a sales role, and you immediately added months to the sales process.

It drives them wild when you allow them to leverage from a position of strength. The smiles on their faces – and the results they produce – are well worth the effort.

LET'S START WITH YOUR STRENGTHS FIRST

One of the best ways to help your people identify their brilliance is to focus on your own strengths first. Once you take yourself through this process, you'll immediately see how it applies to your staff.

What is it that you do well as a leader?

Ah, that question wasn't so easy, was it? The first question we ask our clients is what is it that they do well. Most people have no idea how to answer this question for all the reasons I've stated so far in this chapter, but ask them what they need work in, and they can rattle off a laundry list in a matter of minutes. Is this the same for you?

Here are four strategies you can use to discover your own brilliance.

Use the Brilliant Leader Checklist

The most difficult thing about discovering what you do well is finding the words to describe your brilliance. We're not trained to articulate what we do well because we've been taught not to brag or talk ourselves up. This is not about arrogance, it's about admitting the value you deliver to your company.

Because you're a leader, I want you to focus on what you do well in that role. This checklist, what I call the Brilliant Leader Checklist, is designed to help you articulate your strengths as a leader. Please understand you're brilliant at other things as well, but this will help you hone in on your leadership abilities.

Action step

Take a few minutes to make a checkmark next to the skills you know you have in the Brilliant Leader Checklist below. It's perfectly okay if you only check one item – you can be so masterful at that one area that outweighs everything else. Or you could be pretty good at a lot of things. Check off anything that fits who you are and how you lead. Which skills describe your brilliance?

The Brilliant Leader Checklist

- ☐ I inspire other people to perform at high levels.
- ☐ I'm a good listener. I hear the meaning between the words.
- ☐ I see the potential in other people.
- ☐ I value differences in style, skills, approaches and backgrounds.
- ☐ When chaos is swirling all around me, I have the capacity to figure out what really matters. And only do that.
- ☐ I see the world beyond where we are. I'm great at predicting the future.
- ☐ I know how to create a sense of urgency to get things done – and I know when to stop.
- ☐ People tell me I have a great sense of humor. My people love working with me because we laugh all the time.
- ☐ I advocate for my people within the system. They know they can depend on me.
- ☐ I know how to work the system to get things done.
- ☐ I remove obstacles so my people can do what they do best: their jobs.
- ☐ I create a supportive environment where my team feels safe to take risks and be themselves. We don't shoot messengers around here.
- ☐ I do whatever it takes to get the job done in a way that honors people.
- ☐ I can make tough decisions when they need to be made.
- ☐ I have great capacity to tell the truth in a graceful and respectful way.
- ☐ I create powerful relationships wherever I go.
- ☐ I easily integrate my work with my life.

☐   I am comfortable in my own skin, and I bring that authenticity out in others.

☐   I am compassionate and sensitive to other people's feelings.

☐   I put people at ease. They know they can say anything to me without feeling judged.

☐   I am flexible and open to new ideas.

☐   I can pull seemingly contradictory skillsets and various personalities together to build a high-performing team.

☐   I have strong negotiation skills. My motto is win–win.

☐   I insist on collaborating with people who are smarter than I am. I respect and appreciate the power of the group.

☐   People make fun of me because I plan out everything. It's rare that something goes wrong on my watch.

☐   I take complex concepts and communicate them in a simple effective way.

☐   I know I'm a master communicator. People listen to what I have to say in all venues.

☐   I'm great with numbers and know how to use them to our advantage.

☐   Most people trust and believe me. They know I stand strong in my character and values.

☐   I exude positive energy. People naturally want to be around me.

☐   I'm detail oriented. I can take big ideas and make them real.

☐   I'm great at herding cats. I can facilitate group discussion on any issue.

☐ I am a great coach. The people around me always strive to be the best they can be.

☐ I can take two or three unrelated ideas and create something incredible.

Ask five people

Because you've been trained to focus on your weaknesses, it's hard as heck to identify what it is you do well. I've found most people need to get other people involved in this process because they can see what you can't. A wise man once told me, "You can't see your blind spots." And he's right. We often can't see what we're good at.

Who do you want to ask for help with this? I recommend you ask five people who know you well, have seen you in action as a leader and have the capacity to tell you the truth. There are many people in your life who will tell you what you want to hear. In this case, you need a handful of people who will tell you what you need to know. Make sure you select folks who will tell you the truth no matter what that is.

And when they start talking about what you don't do well, you must immediately stop them in their tracks and say, "No, we're talking about strengths here. We can focus on weaknesses at another time." Be strong and hold yourself to a high standard to get the feedback you need.

Action step

Sit down this week with five people who have the capacity to give you the feedback you need. Ask them, "What is it I do well?" Then sit back and listen to their responses. Don't judge what they have to say; instead, take it in and start owning what are your natural strengths. How can you use this information to get even better results with team? Come up with one idea and apply it this week.

Hire an executive coach

A well-trained executive coach may be the perfect person to call in to help you with this activity. My team has gone through hours of training to master their skills in helping clients not only identify their brilliance, but leverage from a position of strength. You may want to hire one to help you individually and then leverage those skillsets to get better results.

Remember that your strengths are often your blind spots because you take them for granted. They are so much a part of you, you don't realize how valuable they are. A good coach will be able to flush out what strengths you can use right away to get strong results.

Pay attention to how you show up as a leader

When you begin grasping the power of this philosophy, you will naturally start paying attention to what you're good at – and what you're not so great at. But I want you to step this up to a whole new level. Pretend that you're an observer in your life who's sole responsibility is to identify what you're naturally gifted at doing. What activities come easily and naturally? Where do you get the most recognition? What are people constantly telling you that you're talented at performing?

Take the time to capture these thoughts in your planner or Palm Pilot, and start watching for trends. What are the skills that show up again and again? Great leaders leverage from a position of strengths, not from weakness.

COMMUNICATING WHAT YOU'RE NOT GOOD AT

The best leaders I know have one thing in common: they're real, genuine and comfortable in their own skin. The biggest benefit you'll get by designing your work around what you do well is you can let go of your obsession with trying to be something you're not.

Most leaders in today's fast-paced world not only have the responsibility of managing a team, but they must also perform to a certain level. Top salespeople are selling and managing a team. Highly trained technical folks are troubleshooting problems while leading a team of engineers. Gone are the days when you can be the leader and nothing else. That fact makes this do what you do best philosophy even more important.

Let's go back to Andy, the client I told you about a few pages ago. When Andy first start uncovering his strengths, there was a quiet fear that came as well. He was concerned that if he didn't try to cover up his weaknesses, other people would use them as a weapon against him. They would see a vulnerability and attack at that weak place.

An excellent point, I told him. There is just one problem with this line of thinking: you don't have to be the best at everything as the leader. That's what your people are there to do. If you hire the right people and put them in the right roles, you'll get the coverage, intellect, expertise and skills you need to be masterful in the market. Andy was falling back into the trap of believing he had to do everything himself. He secretly believed he had to know the answers and never admit he didn't have a decision made. Old economy thinking.

> **Think of how freeing it would be to admit that you're good at some things – and not so good at others. I know in my own life, this has been a huge leap for me. And a rewarding one.**

When I first starting writing my column, I was caught up in writing only about subjects I had mastered myself. I wrote success stories, strategies that worked and problems I overcame. I didn't want to show that I wasn't perfect, so I wrote about things that would make me look good. My column was well-received, but not overwhelming successful.

Then my dear friend and coach at the time, Madeleine Homan, told me I needed to write more from my heart. She gave me the assignment of reading a book that was full of spirit, and I was crying (in a good way) fifty pages into it. The author, Jack Kornfield, wrote with compassion and love that came out in every word mostly because he admitted his own mistakes. He shared his experiences of when he had taken a wrong turn or behaved badly, and his vulnerability touched me in a profound way.

The very next week I wrote about a major failure I had experienced. Up to that point, I would get a response or two every week from readers who enjoyed my work. That week? You got it. I received more than 100 emails from readers who were touched by my words. They were impacted by my ability to be authentic, to admit where I had made a wrong turn, and they felt for the first time as if I was writing especially to them. My column got picked up by business papers all over the United States in a matter of weeks. Yes, simply because I chose to be who I am in my writing.

What would happen if you freed yourself from being someone you're not? Your people will feel a connection to you that hasn't existed up to this point. Loyalty matters in today's economy, and being comfortable in your own skin is the sign of the most influential of leaders.

Action step

It's time to give up trying to be something you're not. This week I want you to admit to your team that you know you're not good at this thing or the next. No, this isn't a pity party. It's a "Will you take over this project area as you're much more suited for this than I am?" comment rather than a "I'm a lazy bum" statement. See the difference?

A crucial skill to learn as a leader is to stop trying to be everything to everyone. Your need to be right most of the time drives a huge wedge between you and your people, and you're preventing them from shining by hogging the spotlight for yourself. Know what you're good at, and let your team take over in all the other areas.

There's an old adage that says, "The best leaders hire people who are smarter than they are." That statement is so true, and it's up to you to admit when you need their help.

NOW ON TO YOUR PEOPLE

It's one thing to know what you shine at doing, it's quite another to coach your people to own their strengths.

I remember I was sitting in a coffee shop years ago with a friend of mine. We were talking about this do what you do best philosophy, and Pat said to me, "What do you see as my greatest strength?" Now Pat is the type of woman who plans ahead. When you go to her house and open her cupboards, she has three years worth of canned foods ready to be opened. Me? We rarely have enough food to last us a week. Pat is organized and constantly thinking about what's going to go wrong so she can solve the problem before it arises.

Yet when I shared with her what I saw, she replied, "Isn't everyone this way?" Ah, I don't think so. You have to remember that your people may have a hard time owning what they're good at doing. Be patient as you help them uncover what they do well as it will probably take some time for them to integrate this philosophy in their work.

You can speed up the process by putting them in positions to use their strengths – and then be sure to reward, acknowledge and recognize when they perform at high levels. It's amazing what people will continue to do when they get recognition for a job well done.

Action step

Set an appointment with each one of your direct reports for the sole purpose of helping them identify what they do well. You may want them to read this chapter in the book so they get a better idea of what you're trying to do. When they walk out of your office, be sure they're walking away with one specific activity they will be doing that week to leverage from their strengths areas. You need to start using their talents right away, so think ahead on what each person can do to put this philosophy into action.

REDESIGNING THE WORKLOAD

Here comes the tricky part: aligning their responsibilities and outcomes to real company results based on strength areas. Most leaders will not immediately redesign an entire department simply because they identified their employees' strengths. They've spent too much time investing in organizational charts to do that. Nor would I want you to redesign your company on individuals. Smart organizational design is based on certain jobs that need to be done to get results. What this strengths philosophy is all about is making sure you leverage the strengths of the people you have in these roles. Let's take it slow.

As I stated before, this process takes time. What you can do today to get better results based on what your people do well? Focus on what matters and how those skills impact the team's performance – and your bottom line. Retaining your staff and having them feel good about themselves in one thing. Doing that and producing results, that's the real quest.

Action step

Many employees feel overloaded with their current workload, and you certainly don't want to add to their stress by giving them more to do. I recommend you make a list with your team of the major initiatives currently underway along with who's currently responsible for that area. Is there someone in the group who's either (1) better suited for the role or (2) can jump in to off load some of the work? Give people a little room to volunteer in areas they know they shine at doing and measure the results based on their performance.

As you become more comfortable with aligning strengths with results, you'll start to seek out the right people – and more importantly, they'll start to seek out opportunities themselves.

A WORD OF CAUTION

You need to be extra careful that you don't pigeonhole your people into one area of strength. In today's economy, constant stimulation is the name of the game, and your top talent will not be satisfied doing the same activities day after day. Imagine what your work would be like if you did one thing for eight hours every day.

Designing the workload around strengths does not mean you don't give your people an opportunity to develop and grow. Many times we discover things about who we are when we put ourselves in different situations. Keep in mind that you want to give your people an opportunity to shine at what they do well. Help them become masterful at what they are talented at already and from there you can help them develop new skills.

Think about it this way: Michael Jordan was a master at basketball. Every day he focused on improving his game to an even higher level. Yet one morning he decided he wanted to play baseball. Because he was gifted at basketball and well-known in that field, he could easily try out a new game without it impacting his basketball game. Michael played baseball, had fun and ultimately went back to where he felt most at home: the basketball court. Your people want the same thing. Once they know they're coming from a position of strength, they can experiment with new behaviors or situations. If they learn a new skillset, all the better. If they don't, the change wasn't too risky because they can fall back on their natural strength areas. And results won't be impacted because of their experiment.

It's easier to try new things when you've already mastered something else.

THE POWER OF BRILLIANCE

I had the great pleasure of coaching a former senior vice president of human resources for many years. Denny and I used to sit in his coffee shop (the entrepreneurial life he chose after years of corporate jobs) and talk about the challenges leaders face. He would often say to me, "Jen, many leaders show up like real jerks, but the truth is they walk around with so much arrogance because they're trying to cover up that they don't believe they're good enough."

Being a leader forces you, I think, to be a psychologist. If human capital is the key to a successful future, you need to learn how to harness that power and overcome what blocks them from being brilliant. I'm not suggesting that you go back to college and get a psychology degree. But here's what I know: your people are walking around with self-esteem issues that impact their performance and ultimately your results.

> **When you become a catalyst to help them discover what's brilliant about them, you do more for their self-esteem than anything else. And when their self-esteem improves, so do the results.**

Everyone of us needs people to tell us how amazing we are. Are you serving that role for your people?

IT DRIVES THEM CRAZY WHEN . . .

1. All you do is highlight what they're not doing well.
2. You keep setting the bar higher and higher in areas that don't come easily to them. They have to struggle to get results.
3. You tell them to create well-balanced careers. They do and don't get promoted because they're just like everyone else.
4. You take the great assignments even though there is someone else is better suited for that responsibility.
5. They think they aren't shining at their work because of their own inadequacies. And they're even more annoyed when they realized you did this to them.
6. You pretend that you're good at everything.
7. You pigeonhole them into one area and never let them try something new.
8. You don't value the strengths they bring to the team.

9.   You try to get everyone to follow the career path you took.

10.   You never tell them how amazing they are.

IT DRIVES THEM WILD WHEN . . .

1.   You allow them to leverage from a position of strength.

2.   You tell them to set aside their weaknesses and focus on being masterful in natural skill areas.

3.   You let them focus on the work that they can do well. And you acknowledge the impact they make.

4.   You match assignments to skillset.

5.   You let them know what you're personally good at doing – and where you need their help. Then you let them shine.

6.   You give them the freedom to try new things but only after they've mastered a skillset. Risk isn't so terrifying when they come from a position of strength.

7.   You honor different career paths, and you do your best to aid them in that quest.

8.   You know that how you were managed won't work in today's economy.

9.   You value a wide variety of skillsets and talents.

10.   You tell them how amazing they are. Over and over again.

CHAPTER #6

Communicate with power

One of my clients said something that struck a chord with me recently. Chris had called to apologize for missing our coaching session (even the most organized among us have to reschedule from time and time), and he was giving me a quick update on activities that week. He said, "Jen, do you remember a year ago when you told me a key growth is to learn how to communicate? Well, I'm ready. It's time to tackle my communications issues." I love it when my clients step up and want to take on the hard stuff. Communications is one of those things. It's seen as part of the soft skills, but it's vital to driving results, inspiring your team and feeling as if you're moving in the right direction.

N TODAY'S ECONOMY where everything moves at warp speed and there are thousands of pieces of data to digest, it's your job as a leader to communicate in a powerful way. And do it fast.

The problem is most leaders don't even have fundamental communications skills to work with their staff let alone the high-level skillset today's leaders must have at their fingertips.

Which brings me back to my client Chris, the owner of a small yet extremely successful financial planning company. For the past year, he's been experiencing employee turnover issues that started when he let a key employee go. They had outgrown each other, and Chris was facing the challenge of taking his business in a new direction. The marketplace was demanding that he change, and for his own sanity, Chris needed to do something different with his business.

That task wasn't as easy as he originally thought it would be. When is it ever? He soon realized is his long-term employee had learned how to interpret what he truly meant when he said something. There's this flow you get in with someone after five years, and Chris underestimated how much he didn't have to communicate with her. They got to the point when they could finish each other sentences, and she anticipated his every move.

Chris kept hiring new administrative people, and when they weren't performing quickly, he'd let them go. I coached him see that he was a huge part of that problem because he didn't take the time to communicate the way the new team needed him to. He fell into the trap of believing they should be able to anticipate his every move although they'd only be with him less than a month. Old habits are hard to break.

So when Chris told me he was finally ready to improve his communications skills, I immediately replied, "Chris, this is perfect timing. I'm writing the 'Communicate With Power' chapter this month for my new book." To which he said, "Jen, I don't need to learn how to communicate with power. I need to learn how to communicate *with kindness.*"

That one statement stopped me in my tracks. Communicating with kindness is what most of my clients need. In our chaotic, I-wanted-it-yesterday world, we could all use a little more kindness. Me included.

I believe the word power reflects what you as the leader want. What do you think of when you hear the word power? For most people, it means exerting control over someone else. It means being better than, more influential, strong. Images come to mind of a controlling, cruel overseers cracking whips at their slaves. Force and abuse are rampant in our minds when we use the word power.

When I use the word, "power," it means being who you are as a leader. Being authentic, genuine and standing tall in who you are. It means you're powerful not over other people, but with other people.

According to the dictionary, power means the ability or capacity to perform and the strength or force exerted.

I think there's an even better definition out there. There's a fella Charlie Kreiner, the founder of the Institute for Diversity Education in America, who describes power in such a profound way. His definition of power is having the ability to create, nurture and sustain life in all its diversity. It's a regenerative power rather than a traditional power.

What a great way to see power in today's economy. Regenerative, evolving and constantly growing. Are you communicating in a way that regenerates and become even more powerful as it's passed along?

Chris was right. Power has everything to do with kindness. It has everything thing to with being polite and gracious. It has everything to do with putting ideas in the world that regenerative when you're no longer around. Strong leaders often leave a legacy with the people they've worked with, and communicating with power is where it all starts.

WHY IS COMMUNICATIONS SO IMPORTANT?

Most leaders I work with do a tremendous job of creating a vision for their team, but they do a poor job of communicating that message in order to get better results. Leaders focus on the "what," but their employees want to know "how" to make the vision real. And leaders simply don't know how to articulate this. They instead say things like, "That's why I hired you. You figure it out." An employee walks away frustrated and unable to produce the results they both want. Worse, the leader blames the team when things go wrong.

Let me use an analogy to explain this. Pretend that you're standing on the edge of a cliff on top of a huge mountainous area. You're standing in the New World. Right across the ravine is another cliff called the Old World where your employees live. There's a bridge that connects the Old World to the New World. As a leader, you want your employees to be in your world, the New World. This is where you want to play. It's exciting in your world, full of possibilities, innovations and huge profits. But your employees are stuck in the Old World, in the old way of doing things, and you desperately want them to cross the bridge and join you in your way of thinking.

What most leaders do is stay in the New World trying to get their team's attention. They jump up and down screaming, but the wind at the top of these mountains make it hard to hear. So they just yell louder yet still no one is listening. Eventually they get frustrated. You hear these leaders say things like, "No matter what I do, they just don't hear me," or "I'm never going to get them to change," or "They just don't get it. I need to find better employees."

Has it ever occurred to you that the answer is not to yell, scream and wave your arms? Instead, why don't you walk across the bridge into the Old World, take your employees by the hand and lead them over the bridge to the New World?

That's what Chris had failed to do with his team. He failed to go into the old way of thinking and help bridge the gap into the New World. I know you're doing this, too. More mistakes are made not because employees don't get it, but because you didn't take the time to communicate what you want them to achieve.

I remember one day I was coaching Chris, and he began ranting and raving about how one of his employees had let him down. If you're a leader in your organization, I'm sure you've experienced this before. You delegate a project to someone, and they screw it up. It is annoying, and you probably got angry. Chris was fuming.

A few months ago, Chris decided to find someone to duplicate his efforts. No, not so he could delegate projects to someone. He already had office staff to handle those tasks. Chris went out to find a clone of himself so he could triple his company's production without spending more time doing it himself. He hired a fella we both thought could do the job.

During his new employee's training, Chris was very careful to test this person before giving him the most important activities. When he thought his staff person was ready, Chris gave the most crucial part of his business away: the financial piece. And that's where it all broke loose.

While Chris was complaining to me that day, I calmly asked, "How much time did you spend teaching him how to complete this important task?" To which Chris said, "That's not the point! He screwed up the most important part of my business." I said again, "Okay, I get that. But how much time did you spend explaining what your expectations were?" The answer I got was five minutes.

Chris spent less than five minutes training his employee how to handle the financial elements of his business. Five minutes! Yet Chris' response was: "But Jen, he should have known. That's why I pay him as much as I do. He's supposed to know how to do these things."

Supposed to know? How? How on earth would Chris' employee know how to do something if he was never told what the performance expectations were? You can see why Chris soon got quiet and realized he was a big part of the problem.

If you want to produce amazing results in your organization, you need to become a master communicator. Now I didn't say a master manipulator. I'm not going to insult your intelligence and teach you all the ways you can manipulate your team to do what you want. I stand for authentic leadership: how to be who you are and communicate in a powerful way so your team joyfully follows you.

In my work with executives, I believe communicating with power comes down to this one equation:

Strategic Intention + Message + Personal Style + Authenticity + Consideration

×

Trust

= Master Communicator

YOUR STRATEGIC INTENTION, THE "WHAT"

It won't do us any good to focus on how to bridge the gap until we define what this New World means for you. Now rather than taking the time to create a huge vision for you and your company – I said earlier that most leaders I know already have an idea of where they're headed – we're going to identify one major result you want to produce in the next twelve months. This is what I call your strategic intention. It's something you as the leader can see happening. Some people call this your vision of where the company is going. I like the words Strategic Intention because it means (1) you're going somewhere that's strategic and ties in with what your company is truly about, and (2) it's your intention to make this dream of yours real.

> **Do you know where your company is headed? The reason I ask that question is I've always believed that most leaders have a compelling vision for their business. Where they have problems is they don't communicate it in a powerful way to their people.**

I think maybe I was wrong.

I was having lunch with some clients the other day to discuss how we were going to package coaching for their key technical leaders. Two of the men I was with work in partnership to lead and grow their IT consulting firm. Their small company is in the midst of exploding, going through what I call hypergrowth, and they're gearing up to take advantage of the great opportunities. What an exciting time for everyone involved.

Over lunch, I was sharing with them this new communications model I recently created when we got to the concept of strategic intention. Okay, so I didn't even get to the rest of the model because a leader starts with what they're trying to create. Unless you know where you're going, you're never going to get there. But heck, you already know that.

Dave looks at Scott and says, "We know what our vision is, don't we?" The next thing I know they're in a heated discussion on exactly what their strategic intention is. Two minutes later, we all laughed and Dave says to me, "I think we need some work in this area."

Developing a strategic intention is one of the most important things you do as a leader. I'm not talking about goal setting where you put down in writing specific accomplishments you want the team to achieve. No, having a strategic intention is about projecting out into the future and having a mental picture of what tomorrow will look like. Vision is always about greatness. It's having an acute sense of the possible. It's about dreaming the big dream, knowing that despite the hardships your team will face, this is why you're doing what you're doing.

Most people say, "I want to live my life day by day and see what happens." What happens then is mediocrity or worse, heated discussions over lunch because no one fully agrees on where you're headed. Unless you give your people a reason to follow you, they won't. It's too easy for them to get caught up in the new gadget that's supposed to make them more productive or a cool new web site where they can post messages about the horrid things their managers did to them. Without a strategic intention, stories about you will probably show up on that site.

How do you find your strategic intention? It means you get out of the office, put aside your work for a day and let yourself day dream. What shows up about the future when you let your mind wander? Some people go on vision quests where they head out to the woods without food or water for forty-eight hours. Other people dream in their back yards, at a luxurious spa, anywhere but the office.

If you're running an organization with someone else, take them with you. I once had two clients who were so interested in this idea, they locked themselves in a hotel room for an entire weekend vowing not to leave until their vision was in writing and they both agreed. Yes, they left with something incredibly compelling that still drives their company today.

Just don't fall into the trap of including too many people in this process. Strategic intention is really a dictatorial process. That's one of the most valuable things you bring to the table as the leader: knowing exactly where the team is going. And many times you're the only one who can develop this.

It's important to note that you may have had an intention a few years ago that bores you today. Or perhaps you've already made that vision a reality. Don't be afraid to change direction or focus. When I started my business, my first goal was to build a company that would support my lifestyle. Truth be told, all I really wanted was to be able to pay my mortgage and never have to get another job. I outgrew that vision pretty darn quick. And you will, too. When you first start this process, you'll probably only be able to project out a year or two. As you practice your skills, you'll find yourself having bigger ideas and dreams to support company growth for a much longer time.

All I know is it's time to dream. It's time to put yourself out there and decide what you really want. Your people will thank you, and so will your business.

Action plan

What is your strategic intention for the next twelve months? Think about the areas you'd most like to impact and the results you want your team achieve. What do you intend to accomplish as a team in the next year? Get your strategic intention on paper, and start sharing it with your team. They need to know where they're headed as much as you do.

WORD OF CAUTION

Your strategic intention isn't a mission statement. I'm not asking you to sit down and identify a mission statement for your company, your department or even for your life. In fact, I want you to stop spending time on those darn mission statements.

Okay, I know. This is going against what every business book tells you, but it's time someone told you the truth. As an executive coach, I've spent many days inside large and small companies. What I often see when I walk in the reception area of most companies are pretty frames on the wall with a mission statement. Yes, I always take the time to see what's written. Doesn't everyone?

Then I sit down with the CEO or high-level executive. Guess what?

Very few companies ever follow what's on the wall. I typically ask what their mission has to do with the way they're running their business. I often I get some long oratory about how they spent thousands of dollars with some consultant who came in and got the entire organization involved in developing a few pretty words. It took months, they tell me. Hours upon hours of meetings. Weekend retreats. Every single word analyzed and reviewed. Their mission statement must be worth something if it took that long to create.

But is it really? Not very often, in my opinion. It looks good on the wall, but these mission statements are not reality.

Being a powerful leader means you must have a vision of what you're trying to accomplish. You need to have some end result, some way of measuring performance. Business is about profit and results, after all. But when I tell you to throw away your mission statement, it doesn't mean I'm telling you to stop creating big dreams for your company. Fundamentally, as the company leader, that's your job: to be the dreamer.

Placing some pretty words in a frame has nothing to do with honoring your staff. It has nothing to do with listening to them. And it has nothing to do with creating a big dream for your company. You need to stop wasting company resources to develop these statements, whether you call them value statements or vision statements or whatever. They're all the same in my book.

To create that strategic intention to guide you during the next year, step back and ask yourself three important questions:

1. "What really matters to me as the leader?"

The first step in creating a strategic intention is for you decide what's important to you. If you're not getting what you need from your career, you'll never be happy no matter what result you produce. Yes, it's perfectly okay to tell me that what you want is to make a lot of money. Better to be honest than lie to yourself. I've seen too many leaders put aside what they want and instead focus only on company needs. If you're not jazzed about the outcome, why do it?

Go on. Write down what really matters to you as the leader.

2. "What really matters to my customers?"

This is not to say that your customers are always right. They're not. But it's crucial that you know what your customers expect from you. Is it a high-quality product? Real-time service? Innovative ideas? Again, you don't need these words on the wall. You need to talk to your customers to get the answers. Are you?

Go on. Write down what really matters to your customers, the people who ultimately pay your salary.

3. "What really matters to my staff?"

One of my clients – I'll call him Wayne – is in the midst of starting yet another business. With his other business, one that made the Inc. 500 list, he focused on fast growth. "Grow, grow, grow!" was his mantra no matter what the cost. What suffered in his quest for growth was his profitability, and he lost some key employees in the process.

This time he wants to do it differently. His No. 1 priority is making sure he creates a corporate culture that enables the spirit of his employees. Wayne knows that if his employees are doing what they do best, if they're leveraging their own individual strengths, nothing will stop the company's performance. But he doesn't need words on the wall for his employees to get what he's creating. They know because they live it every single day.

Go on. Write down what really matters to your employees.

You don't need pretty words to tell me the answers to these questions. What you need is to take action against what truly matters, what I've called your strategic intention.

Develop strategic, workable plans that will get the job done. Hold your staff accountable for their performance and reward them in a variety of ways when they deliver. And it's definitely your job to anticipate future needs of your customers, so they stay customers for a long time. Yes, yes, all the stuff I've taught you in this book.

Real leadership comes from results, not finding words to put on the wall.

Only the bold leaders tell me their mission statement has nothing to do with how they run their businesses. They're the ones who march into the reception area to take the mission statement off the wall and throw it away. They understand that results– not words – matter.

Today I want you to be one of the bold ones. You do that by identifying what your strategic intention is – what you want your people to strive to be – and then lay in a course of action to make it real.

YOUR COMPELLING MESSAGE

Once you've decided what your strategic intention is, you need to whittle it down into a compelling message to use for the next 90 days. What do you want your employees to know about what they're trying to accomplish? Yes, what you're trying to achieve is a pretty good place to start. Why you're going for that goal is another important thing.

Again, this is not a bunch of flowery words. You take your strategic intention and you ask yourself, "What message do I need to communicate to inspire my team to get us closer to this goal?" If you develop messages for 90-day cycles, you won't sound like a broken record.

Remember, one of the major challenges you're experiencing as a leader is overloaded employees. If you're operating in a fast-paced, constantly changing world, you need to develop a message that's compelling, something your people will remember, a message to keep them on course. It's always simple, easy to remember, and it touches a special place in their hearts.

The truth is a crucial element when crafting your compelling message. The one thing I've loved about working with dot-com leaders is how authentic they are. As one of my clients said, "Make no mistake about it. We're in this to make a buttload of money. I know it. Our customers know it. Our employees know it. And they're all here to make more money." You probably can figure out what my clients' compelling message is just from this statement. Brutal honesty works.

Here are the steps to follow to create a compelling message.

Step 1: what message do you want to send?

Go back to your strategic intention and identify what your team needs to achieve as a group in the next 90 days. If your strategic intention is to become a world-class sales organization within the next year, what accomplishments do you need in the next three months? The answer is the beginning your message.

Step 2: make it compelling

To make your message compelling, you then need to think about what's in it for your people. Are you rewarding them with a big bonus or team trip at the end of the quarter if they reach their goals? Will beating the competition charge them up? Your message is a combination of what they want and what you want.

What do they need to hear that will inspire them to reach new heights? That's the compelling part.

Action step

For the next week, I want you to pay attention to every advertising message you see. Yes, every one of them. I told you earlier in the book that I used to work in corporate marketing and I married an advertising guy. We know an awful lot about compelling messages in my household. When my husband Steve was in advertising, we used to drive around town and look at the billboards. Who was doing a good job capturing our attention? Who put way too much information on their boards? Which one did we completely disregard because they were just plain dumb?

Jot yourself some notes in your Palm Pilot or in your planner on which messages impacted you and why. Did you go for ones that were emotional and heart warming or ones that were more hard-hitting? You'll start to get a sense of your own personal style by paying attention to what you like and don't like.

Step 3: act like an advertiser does

There's a statistic in advertising that has guided me with my clients. According to the industry research, it takes someone three to thriteen times before they take action based on your message. Yes, I did say three to thirteen times. Someone needs to see a McDonald's television commercial for the new Monopoly promotion at least three times before they rush to their local McDonald's to participate. For many of us, we need to see and hear the same thing thirteen times before we do anything about it.

How many times do you drive by a new retail store in your neighborhood before you stop and check it out? All good advertisers know running one ad never works. You have to hit them over and over again.

Use this same line of thinking with your employees. They need to experience your message at least three times before they do anything with it. Most leaders make the mistake of sharing their goals or strategic intentions once with their team at the annual staff retreat. When you have 200 emails to read, deadlines you're trying to meet and your phone's ringing off the hook, who can remember the boss' goals for the year? Yes, no one. Being a masterful communicator means saying the same thing multiple times many different ways.

If you're trying to completely change the course of your business, be prepared to share your thoughts with them numerous times. People are naturally slow to integrate new ideas, and they need this repetitiveness of your message. Pretend you're a broken record saying the same thing over and over again. It's amazing how your words will become part of their psyche if they hear it enough.

Action step

Once you've crafted your compelling message, it's time to decide how you're going to communicate this with your team. First, make a list of at least twenty-five different ways you can articulate your 90-day message. Don't be wimp and only write out one or two different ways to say the same thing. Make a list of twenty-five different ways to communicate your message.

Then create an action plan on how you're going to use that message during the next three months. Ask your coach – or a colleague – to hold you accountable for this action plan. Good communications takes work, and you must invest the time if you want to get better results.

APPLY YOUR PERSONAL STYLE

Ah, your personal style. Communicating in a way that you feel comfortable and genuine is a crucial part of being a master communicator. That's what we call your personal style.

Take a moment to remember some of the best leaders you've worked for in the past. Each one of them had a different style, I imagine, and each one touched you in a different way.

When looking at the way leaders communicate, we primarily see four main styles. Of course, you can have a combination of each style to fit different situations – and we want you to develop a wide spectrum of styles. But you first have to decide where you are today and then you can integrate different styles based on which audience you're trying to impact.

Different communications styles

Directive style

You typically say this is how things will be without too much two-way communications with your team. You typically come up with the goal, pull the team together and help them execute against it. Your style reflects your direct, to-the-point attitude.

Interactive style

You love asking for feedback and involving yourself in dialogue with your team. You ask lots of questions and create a very democratic environment where a wide range of opinions are heard. You communicate in a way that allows everyone to have a say in what's being done.

Inspiring style

Your people will follow you anywhere because you have high energy and are enthusiastic. People are drawn to you, and they've told you that you inspire them with your passion.

Analytical style

You approach communications in a logical fashion. You like to use PowerPoint presentations and lots of details to make sure everyone understands the what, how and why of every situation. It's rare you lose your cool under pressure.

Once you understand what natural communications style you use, you can start to own who you and what you're all about. If the situation requires a more analytical speaker and you love to talk from your heart, you can delegate this responsibility to someone on your team. Masterful communicators know who they are and who they're not, and they use that as an advantage when communicating with the people around them.

Action step

Before you communicate your compelling message, ask yourself these important questions:

1. What is your natural communications style?

2. What style is needed for the message you need to communicate in order to get the right results from your team?

3. Is there a match between your style and what your message demands? If not, what are you going to do to compensate for this challenge?

BE AUTHENTIC

Authenticity is perhaps the most difficult of the six elements to measure, but it's definitely the most important.

What beliefs do you hold about who a leader is? The reason I ask that question is who you believe you need to be gets in the way of who you are. And that mucks up how you communicate. Let me give you an example. I'm very much an inspiring and directive communicator. I'm full of energy, and I love to deliver in-your-face messages to audiences I have the pleasure of speaking with. I talk fast, and I expect people to get caught up in my passion and enthusiasm.

That's what I know about myself today. But when I was a young executive, I had a complex that I was too young to be a leader. I believed the best leaders were middle aged white men who had years of experience. I saw them communicate in very analytical ways so that's what I thought I had to do. I set aside my personal power to be someone I'm not. And guess what? Yes, mediocre results.

For years, people would get just a little bored when I communicated with them. I had positional power in my role in the company, but I didn't have personal power. Why? Because I wasn't being authentic to who I am and what I bring to the world. I was too busy playing a role and wearing a mask. I was afraid to speak the truth and own that I was – still am – a young, white, feisty, direct, on the edge, fireball of a woman who has a lot to say.

It took many years to show up in an authentic way as a leader. I didn't want to admit I don't have all the answers. I was afraid people would think I'm out of my mind or worse, flighty and stupid. But let me tell you, not being who I am was burden-some. It's hard to walk around trying to be something you're not. When push comes to shove, your people admire and respect who you are, not the face you put on to the world. People today are smart. They can see through the smoke screens, and they expect you to be truthful, authentic and comfortable in your own skin.

Are you?

Action step

I'm a big fan of journalling, and this authenticity question is the ideal journal assignment. Write this question at the top of the page: What's different about who you are at work verses who you are when you're at home? Then let your pen take off and write for three pages. This is what we call stream of consciousness journalling. Let your mind go and write down everything that show up in regards to this question. You'll start to uncover where you're wearing a mask and when you're being authentic. Where's the disconnect between who you are and who you're being as a leader?

It's your job as a leader today to work on being who you are all the time. Your people will demand that of you.

HAVE CONSIDERATION

This part of the communications model has everything to do with thinking about who your audience is and what they most need from you. As I've built my business, it's become clear to me that my coaching team needs someone with an interactive style. My team is full of independent thinkers who always have an opinion, and they want an environment that allows them to express their views.

When I was first building the team, I would show up the same every time. I usually have some hot new idea, and I would speed along at a mile a minute sharing this new program or that new strategy. I never slowed down to ask myself if my team was understanding what I was trying to say. It never occurred to me. I figured they were smart enough to figure it out.

You know what happened next. They got easily confused by the massive changes, and they began questioning their roles in what I was creating. As independent thinkers, they wanted to participate in the process, not be dragged along for the ride.

So I had two choices when communicating with them: (1) take on a more interactive style (which I do), and (2) hire a manager who functions well in the interactive style and delegate this responsibility (which I've also done).

It wasn't until I got clear on how I like to communicate – and

what my team needed – that I was able to solve my communications issues. I believe most of our problems stemmed from
my inability to consider who my audience was and what they
needed from me. Instead, I'd tell myself, "I'm a great communicator. My coaches just don't get it." What they didn't get was
what I was saying – and that was my problem, not theirs.

Action step

Before you communicate something important to your
team, step back and consider who they are and what they
need from you. Do they need the minute details in order to
move forward? Will they prefer an overview so they don't
get caught up in too many details? Do they need an emotional, touch-their-hearts message to be inspired? Would
they respond to a more direct, do-it-this-way approach?

Consider who your audience is before you open your
mouth and communicate appropriately. You'll be glad you
did.

TRUST

The reality of the economy today is if your people don't trust
you, it doesn't how passionate you are, how jazzed you are
about your strategic intention, how compelling the message is
and what your communications style is. If they don't trust you,
they won't pay attention to you. If trust levels are low with
your people, you will need to work extra hard. If trust levels are
high, you can skip some of these strategies I've shared with you
on who a masterful communicator is. Your people will forgive
poorly constructed sentences or lengthy meetings if they trust
who you are and what you say – and they'll still produce for

you. But if trust levels are at zero, you will get nothing from them.

1. What kills trust?

Have you ever seen yourself caught up in spinning a story for your team? I often see managers who want to get their staff charged up about what the possibilities are verses what the current reality is, and they spin the facts. It's what we call this hype. Yet what sometimes happens with hype is the staff is left with unmet expectations when things don't turn out as planned.

We're suffering from truth decay. The leaders of tobacco companies know their products are damaging and deny it. Managers who know re-engineering will mean layoffs instead promise no losses and greater opportunities. Supervisors tell an employee he is doing just fine, but the next month he loses his job because his performance wasn't up to par. Larger companies sign year-long contracts with small vendors then break the contract without payment and without reason.

The absence of honesty in the workplace has led to a cynical, skeptical and dispirited workforce. We're in need of revitalization that comes from truly great leaders.

If you want to build greatness in your company, you must inspire trust. When you lie, you betray. Your credibility is lost. Not telling the truth is the source of most problems in your workplace. Yes, truth is fundamental. The more truth, the more success.

Why don't you tell the truth as a leader? Because you don't first tell the truth to yourself. What do we do instead?

Deny

You don't own up to the problem and deal with it. You hire lawyers instead to repair the damage or to render opinions on how much you can get away with. What you're really afraid of is losing your illusion that you're in control. Your lying lets you maintain the illusion. The reality is that by lying, you lose your employees' respect.

Pretend

You often don't tell the truth because you're afraid to show that you too make mistakes. You think being vulnerable means being weak, so you pretend to be strong. You lie. What you forget is that no one will follow you unless they know who you really are. Your team knows when you are pretending, when you are covering up. Your lies lead to mistrust and disrespect.

Control

Excessive rules, policies and procedures breed distrust in an organization. They show your staff that you do not trust them. Excessive rules teach your employees to play the game of how little work they can do and get away with it. You don't trust them, so why should they work hard? If you redirect your energy away from controlling, the trust you create will radically boost morale and success in your workplace.

Delude

Have you even seen a leader who convinces herself that she believes in empowerment, but whose authoritarian behavior is obvious to everybody but herself? Delusion at its best.

When you're so used to your behavior that you no longer really sense the tension it causes. But your body knows. When you tell lies and withhold information, you feel discomfort, neck pain, headache, stomach problems, shortness of breath. The next time you feel physical discomfort, ask yourself what the real truth is that remains unsaid.

In today's world, employees won't put up with this lying anymore. When they catch you spinning too many stories – they will, you know – you'll lose immediate credibility. That means every time you open your mouth to share details with them, they're going to wonder if you're telling the truth.

Action step

Take some time this week to look hard at your own behavior and determine how many lies you tell. Little white lies count. So does the spin control, being tactful, being realistic, telling them only what they need to know. One spin on top of one little lie on top of another leads to big lies. And a big loss of integrity and trust.

Leaders who inspire the souls of others do not treat truth telling lightly. They know trust is easier to lose than to rebuild. They build great relationships founded on honesty, which in turn builds inspired organizations.

Truth restores our energy. And it helps everyone fall in love with work again.

2. What builds trust?

There's one thing that rebuilds trust in an organization: do what you say you're going to do. We've all experienced leaders who ask for feedback, act as if they're deeply listening, promise great things and then do nothing. Besides outright lying to your team, promising action will be taken and then doing nothing crushes their spirits like nothing else. It's the reason they walk around saying things like, "I don't know why they ask." or "They won't do anything with what I have to say." or "Nothing will ever change around here."

Build trust in your organization by following through. Every single time. Great leaders make things happen. They listen, and then they do something about what they're hearing.

Action step

What's one thing you promised your team that you have not yet implemented? Come on, I know there's something on your list that you keep telling yourself you want to do. Now's the time to take action. By the end of the day tomorrow, I want you to accomplish this one thing for your team. And be sure they know what action you took on their behalf. Watch their faces for a reaction. I think you'll be shocked at how surprised they are when you follow through.

WHAT GETS IN YOUR WAY?

Sure, I've given you some great ideas, but what truly stands in your way of communicating with power? Here are the ones I typically hear – and here are some ideas on how to overcome them.

1. You use the time crunch as an excuse.

The biggest excuse I'm always hearing is, "Yeah, Jen, good ideas, but I simply don't have time to spend that much time communicating with my staff. I have results I need to produce."

The bottom line is this: you're using this busyness excuse as just that, an excuse. You always have time for the things that matter the most to you. If your mother was dying of cancer, I know you'd find the time to spend her final hours with her. We make time for the things that truly matter.

So the real question is: What are you afraid will happen if you talk to your people more often?

For most leaders I work with, the answer is control. What's really going on in your head is stuff like:

- If I spend time talking with my team, they'll give me more stuff to do.
- They don't follow along with what I'm saying, and they'll question our direction. And that's just a big fat hassle.
- They'll open up a can of worms I don't want to address.
- I'm just not good at this people thing.
- I'm the boss. Why should I have to explain everything? This isn't a democracy. It's more like a dictatorship.

What's your excuse?

Action step

Go back to Chapter 3 and determine what you're going to let go in order to have enough time to communicate with your staff. If you don't make them a priority, they aren't going to make you a priority. There go your results flying right out the window.

2. You manage by email.

Nothing destroys powerful communications than email.

I recently experienced a major miscommunications with my publicist all because of email, and this problem reinforces my point. Email is a wonderful tool, but you cannot manage your business – or your people – by using it. Not if you want to be a powerful leader.

Celia, my publicist, had just gotten back from a relaxing seven-day vacation in Florida. She opened her email and received a note from me outlining five different things I wanted to talk with her about that week. On my end, I thought I was just giving her a heads-up for a meeting we were going to have. On her end, she misinterpreted my email as an indication that I wanted her to be at my beckon call 24/7. You can see why she immediately called me upset.

This type of thing happens all the time. I see employees sending scathing email on topics they'd never have the courage to say in person. Leaders send replies back infuriated – or worse, they delete the message and say nothing. CEOs send email full of important changes in company policies and then get upset when they find out no one read it. I've even heard of managers firing their workers by email.

Whatever happened to picking up the phone and talking in real time?

Managing by email is a major mistake. It is too easy to misinterpret someone's intention especially as most of us whip out email in about three seconds or less. In today's fast-paced world, most people don't have time to think carefully about what they're writing in an email. Here you are thinking you're helping the situation and all you're doing is starting a conflict that wouldn't be there if you had communicated in an appropriate way.

So here are my top three strategies for leading in today's technocrazy world.

- Only use email for simple topics, not for communicating major issues. That means you use email for scheduling times to meet, sending out agendas, recapping assignments or as a quick "thank you for your time" note. Email is for simple messages only. Do not use it to communicate complex, sensitive or emotional subjects no matter how much you love to write.
- Communicate in a way that works best for the person you're trying to reach. If you want to be heard, you need to spend time thinking about the right way to talk to someone. Does your client or manager prefer email, voicemail or a face-to-face meeting? What voicemail system do they use the most: their office or their cell

phone? Do they want a long oratory from you or to-the-point bullet points?

You wouldn't believe how many times I've heard: "But Jen, he won't call me back!" That's because you're trying to reach that person in a way that isn't easy and convenient for them. Don't fall into the trap of communicating in the way you want to be contacted. Just because you love email doesn't mean everyone else does.

•   Tell people how to best communicate with you.

Let me give you an example. One of my clients – George – is a senior vice president of sales for a Fortune 500 company. A few months back, I was coaching him on how to handle an issue he was facing with one of his employees. This staffer was upset because she always sent George emails full of attachments, and he rarely ever read them. No, not because he was being a jerk. He didn't read them because they were too darn cumbersome to open and read. Invariably, George missed some important points.

I told George that he was at fault because he assumed that his staff knew the best way to communicate with him. But George never told them his preferences. Do you expect your employees to be mind readers? Don't let this be you. Take the time to tell folks how to best reach you.

By taking a few minutes to think about the best way to reach someone, you'll prevent unnecessary conflicts from happening. Please! Stop managing by email.

3. You avoid confrontation at all costs.

Is it just me or do most people have a major problem with confrontation?

My husband and I were having dinner with some friends a few months ago, and after exchanging pleasantries, we started talking about how we really were. My friend John (not his real name) was telling us he was feeling pretty stressed out. He had to fire someone on Monday, and when I asked, "Have you ever let someone go before?" he promptly said, "No." You can see why he was feeling a bit anxious.

Now I have a strict rule that I don't coach my family or my friends, but I couldn't resist asking why he needed to let this fellow go. The story started to take twists and turns, and I ended up in a place I didn't want to be. Let me tell you why.

John had recently taken a job as the director of a huge athletic event. Anyone in sports marketing would kill to have his job. It turns out his sales force – the folks who go out to sell all the sponsorships for this big event – was full of independent contractors. This is often a great way to get aggressive salespeople without having the headaches of hiring employees. One of the guys sent a million-dollar proposal to a potential sponsor without anyone's approval, and John found himself caught up in a situation with a sponsor that made him look bad. The proposal was off by almost $200,000.

Good thing John was new enough in his job that he could play the "I've only been here four months" card so he didn't look like a real fool in front of the sponsor. But John was so upset, he immediately called his attorney to find a way to terminate his sales rep's contract. His lawyer told John to send a letter outlining how he had violated his contract, and their agreement was terminated immediately. John's attorney even recommended that John not call this guy to tell him what to expect, and John was taking his lawyer's advice.

As John's wife said, "Can you imagine sitting at your desk and receiving a letter stating that you've just lost a huge percentage of your income because your contract was terminated? No phone call, no conversation, just a termination letter?" Ugh. I love my attorneys – I really do! – but if they told me to fire someone without an authentic conversation explaining my decision, I'd have to argue with them and find a better way.

I'm sure I don't have all the details of this story, but here's what I know: John was too scared to pick up the phone and tell the truth. He's afraid of confrontation, so he's hiding behind his attorney and a letter. That way John doesn't have to face the pain this type of conversation will undoubtedly bring.

Now don't get me wrong. I'm disputing John's decision to fire this guy. If you can't trust your people to follow the rules and/or make your organization look good, then by all means, find someone else to fill their shoes. What I am disagreeing with is John's decision to hide rather than find the courage to tell the truth. John is a great guy with a big heart, but he obviously has a tremendous problem in having tough conversations.

Why are so many people afraid to have these difficult conversations? Why do we see too many leaders hiding behind lawyers or their gatekeepers? Do you somehow think it's easier to hide than tell the truth?

It's painful to tell someone you're letting them go. It's difficult to tell someone that you don't want to do business with them anymore. It's incredibly hard to tell someone at the office that they let you down. Sending tough news in email or a letter is ridiculous. Not returning phone calls is even worse. Don't you respect yourself enough to face what's really going on?

Because when you refuse to tell the truth – not matter how difficult – that's what you're really doing. You're dishonoring your power as a leader and worse, you're not treating the other person with the respect they deserve. If you were the one being let go, wouldn't you want to hear the real reason your contract was terminated? I know I would, and I know you would, too.

Yes, I did tell John what I thought in a gracious and polite way. At the end of the day, all you really have is your own character and integrity. I'm not sure he will take my advice, but at least I told him what I needed to say.

Action step

What difficult conversation are you avoiding? There's probably someone on your team who isn't performing, and you keep putting off having that conversation. Or perhaps a vendor is letting you down, and you haven't said anything. It's time to address the issues.

Take a few minutes right now to write out the three main things you want to say to the other person. When you get clear on what you want to say, it's a lot easier to have these difficult conversations. Then pick up the phone – or send an email – and schedule a time to meet in person or by phone if they don't live in your city. Stop avoiding confrontation and start telling the truth.

4. You let stress take over. And kindness takes a back seat to getting the work done.

Kindness is precisely what I told Chris he needed to spend some time on if he wanted to communicate with power. No one likes being snapped at or being bossed around. That's exactly what happens when you let stressful situations drive your emotions. No more kindness, only harsh words and accusations.

I know you don't mean to be rude and unkind. But you may be falling into that trap. Go back and follow the actions in this entire book to free up your energy. Powerful leaders know when they're the ones getting in the way.

It's the new time after all. Your people need democratic, open, experimental and flexible work environments. As a leader, you need to give them to them. Are you?

WHAT YOU REALLY NEED TO KNOW ABOUT COMMUNICATIONS

I know it's easy to sit back and blame someone else for your communications issues. We get impatient when our team doesn't blindly follow us. We get annoyed when someone doesn't understand what we're trying to say. There are even days when everyone of us wants to hang out in our caves. Alone.

Yet as a leader, it's your job to be a master communicator. Language is the way you inspire your team. It's the way you influence them to higher levels of performance. Your words have a great impact on your people – either sending them in the right direction or on the spiral down. That's the one thing I've been most amazed with as I've moved into influential leadership roles: how much my words affect the people around me.

If something is that important, doesn't it make sense to spend a huge amount of time learning how to be a master at it? It does to me.

Any time you say something that isn't understood, it's your responsibility to back up and try again. Don't say to yourself, "This person is an idiot." Instead say, "Hmm. Let me try that again." You're the only one who can control what comes out of your mouth. You decide what to say on voicemail, what to write in email and memos. Use your words to show up as a great leader.

Yes, this is a hard thing to do. But your results depend on it.

IT DRIVES THEM CRAZY WHEN . . .

1. You haven't created a strategic intention. Without direction from you, they're lost.
2. You expect them to fully comprehend what you're trying to say when you only say it once. Repetition is good for everyone.
3. You communicate in the way you want to be communicate to. And not the other way around.
4. You pretend to be something you're not.
5. You don't consider their feelings or their communications style when you speak with them.
6. You hide behind lawyers or walls while distorting the truth.
7. You show them you don't trust them by instituting too many rules.
8. You communicate all major news exclusively by email.
9. You avoid confrontation at all costs.
10. You don't communicate with kindness.

IT DRIVES THEM WILD WHEN . . .

1. You communicate a powerful vision that they want to follow.
2. You craft a compelling message that you repeat in many different ways.
3. You are comfortable in your own skin.
4. You speak the truth. Always.
5. You consider their emotions and their position before you open your mouth.
6. You know your communications style, and you can adapt that style to reach different audiences.

7. You address the hard stuff right away.

8. You do what you say you're going to do.

9. You reduce your stress levels as much as you can so you can communicate with kindness the majority of the time.

10. You are a master communicator.

CHAPTER #7

Get a life

Finally, we get to the most important point of this entire book. Getting a life.

I THINK ONE OF YOUR MAIN JOBS as a leader of people is to make sure they get home in time for dinner. Your people cannot be brilliant at work if they haven't taken the time to have a life. When they're at the office, you want them happy, healthy and fulfilled. To do that, they need to replenish, renew and refresh. And the only way to do that is to make sure they have a life.

How do you do that? Make sure *you* have a life. But you're used to that line of thinking by now from me. It all starts with you.

WHY DO YOU WANT TO HAVE A LIFE?

I know you're expecting me to give you this song and dance of why you must give yourself time for a life, why life balance is the answer to lifelong success. Well, I'm not. At least not in the way you think I would. What I am going to do is tell you that the best way to harness the power of your people is to be able to show up as the leader they want you to be almost 100 percent of the time. When you do that, you inspire them to be that good, and they produce the results you want. Then you all win.

You wouldn't believe how many leaders I speak to who are under huge amounts of pressure. It's hard being the boss with so much hitting the desk every minute. When was the last time you walked into someone's office and found it clean and organized? It's been a long time for me, too.

When you're under pressure to hit certain targets, it's also important to give yourself the time and space to rest. You know this intuitively, but I bet here's what is going on in your head. Who has time to do that when your To-Do list is a mile long? When people tell you to slow down, you probably roll your eyes and say to yourself, "Yeah, right. Maybe when that stack on my desk finally goes away." That same feeling of never being caught up is a problem with your team, and it dramatically impacts their performance. How? Because they feel as if they're on a treadmill, and they can't get off.

> **When you're burned out and exhausted, you cannot do your best work. At least not consistently day after day. Sure, you can jam with little sleep for a while, but eventually, it catches up with you.**

The thing that's truly getting in your way is you're so stressed and overworked that you show up like a real jerk sometimes. Come on, you can admit it to me.

When you have too much to do, too many stresses pounding on you that day, it's hard as heck to pay attention to your people when they show up at your door. Your patience levels are low, and you may find yourself getting short or angry over something little. Then watch out. Your people are demoralized, you change plans midstream or worse, come down hard about something that doesn't matter. It's the stress of having too much on the plate that prevents you from being as good as you can be. Think about how edgy, rude and annoying you are to your people when you're under pressure, and you'll understand what I mean.

This happens with me every time I have too much to do. Yes, it's true. I fall back into the same trap you do every once in a while. When I'm stressed out, I start sending short, edgy emails. My staff gets new projects assigned to them with ridiculous deadlines from this micromanaging freak (me) who wants to know every little detail about what's going on. That's my control freak stuff coming out, and I subconsciously think if I can get all the details, I will feel better – I never do. Fortunately, my team has been trained to (1) know I'm not being hateful, but instead stressed out and (2) they ask when I'm going out of town next. I end up laughing at myself when they ask that question because I know what it really means, and we all jump in to reshuffle the workload.

How do you show up as a leader when you're under stress? You may want to review our Stressed Out Leader list to jar your memory. Who would want to work for these people? Yeah, me either.

Stressed Out Leaders Quiz

Here's a list of the things leaders typically do under pressure. Do any of these behaviors describe you?

☐ You bark out orders instead of soliciting input from your team.

☐ You let your ego take over, and you're right all the time.

☐ You push people out of the way and do the work yourself.

☐ You run around like a crazy person to try to get everything done.

☐ You go underground and disappear. You stop interacting with your team, and you try to solve the problems yourself.

☐ You stop doing the outside things that support you.

☐ You stop exercising, going to your kids' soccer games and taking time off.

☐ You start drinking or eating excessively to try to calm yourself down.

☐ You retreat to old habits, old friends and old views.

☐ You start to hesitate on making decisions. Or you freeze.

☐ You stop thinking about the future and put your attention on the crisis right in front of you.

☐ You start withdrawing support of projects you used to support.

☐ You become direct and to the point. In a harsh way.

☐ You're on edge and more impatient than usual.

☐ You start cancelling staff meetings because you don't want to invest the time.

When you're under pressure, your true colors typically show up. It's your job to eliminate the stress so you can be a powerful leader 100 percent of the time. Yes, the answer is get a life. Now.

When you feel good about how you're working – and how you're living – it's easy to be generous, compassionate and inspiring to your team. When you feel crappy about what's going on around you, then you know how you treat your people. And it isn't pretty.

Action step

Take out a sheet of paper and draw a line down the middle of the page. On the left-hand side, write down all the ways you behave when you're under stressed, burned out and overworked. Get everything you do that's not so good down on paper, and don't leave any gory details out. Then on the right-hand side of the page, write out what this behavior does to your team's results. What impact is this not-so-great behavior having on the goals you're trying to achieve?

Yes, this is a tough exercise, but you have to see what not having a life is doing to your performance at the office.

When you're finished with that exercise, identify three things you can add to your life to reduce your stress levels immediately. This may be scheduling a ten-day trek in the woods without your cell phone or laptop. It may be hiring a bill-paying service or personal assistant to handle your personal stresses. Perhaps you need to hire a new nanny, find a cleaning service or persuade your CEO to move some of your workload to another department.

Unless you figure out a way to reduce your own stress levels, you will never get the business results you want. Okay, so that's not true. You may get the results, but you're going to pay too high a price with your people's job satisfaction – and your own happiness.

WHAT IF YOU'RE OKAY WITH HOW YOU'RE LIVING?

Maybe you're reading this telling yourself that you love your work so much you don't mind working those long hours. Perhaps you like your life the way it is, and you believe deep in your heart that you're supposed to work like a dog to get the results you want. Who I am to tell you to change if things are going as well as you say?

But before you close this book and move on, take a look at another reason you have to learn how to get home at a decent hour. If you don't, who will teach your people? As a leader, you need to model good behavior for your people. But what I often see is leaders who don't understand the impact their behavior has on their staff. Something happened to William which is a great example of this. William is an American businessman who was transferred to Japan to run an organization. In the Japanese culture, it's a common rule that no one leaves the office until after the boss does. That's where the problem comes in. William is the type of guy who will get on a roll and work for hours at a time. One evening when he was new on the job, William was in his office working away until 9:30 pm. He went out into the hall to get a Coke, and he noticed that every one of his employees was still in the office working. "How odd," he said to himself as he was walking back to his desk. Then it hit him like a ton of bricks. He was the one influencing their behavior, and they were there because he was.

From then on, when William had the urge to burn the midnight oil, he always left the office at 5 p.m. and went to a coffee shop across the street. He would sit by the window and wait. When he saw the last employee leave the office building – which was typically fifteen minutes after he left – William would go back in and work. What he did was put his people first without impacting his own need to work when he wanted to work.

I want to be clear that I'm not here to tell you that you must reduce your workload to a forty-hour work week. It's your life, and you need to decide how much or how little you want to work. What I am telling you is it's vital that you give your people a choice of how much they want to work. Do not think that they aren't influenced by your behavior. They are. More than you'll ever know.

If they see you working eighty-hour work weeks and sending emails on the weekend, guess what they're going to do? Yes, give up their life to work at the same pace you are. At the beginning of the book I told you a story about Adam, a CEO client of mine who lost his most valued executive because his example was "CEOs have to work way too hard." If you don't learn how to get a life, your people won't either. You set yourself up to lose those people who decide they want to get some balance in their life. They will go find a leader to work for who isn't so obsessed with getting it done no matter how long it takes.

Too many of our high-performing clients shy away from top leadership roles because they didn't see a way to lead and have a life. It is one thing for me to tell them they were the change agents, and if anyone could do it, they could. It's quite another to watch their leaders bust their butts every single day without taking time to invest in what truly matters in life.

Yes, that means your potential leaders won't rise to the occasion. They'll shy away from going for tough assignments, and they'll be satisfied to stay where they are. All because they don't have any solid role models to follow who have proven it's possible to have the top leadership role and a life. Did that every occur to you? By watching your behavior, your people are not compelled to follow in your footsteps. Look at how you're living. Would anyone want to be you?

Please do not sit there and tell me your people understand that you may work as hard as you do, and it's okay if they don't. They won't believe you no matter how many times you tell them you want them to have a life. They believe your actions, not your words.

If you're not willing to get a life for yourself, then by all means, do it for them. It'll drive them wild to see you loving your life as much as you love your work. They'll strive to follow in your footsteps then, and that will in turn drive you wild.

Action step

The next time you decide to read email on weekends or respond to voicemail on Sunday afternoon, ask yourself: What example am I setting for my team? If it's an example you want to set, then continue moving forward. If it's not something you would encourage them to do – like giving up their weekend to work – then take a few minutes and choose a different path.

What would you tell them to do with their weekend? Follow your own advice.

YOUR COMPELLING REASON

I just laid out two reasons you may want to get a life: (1) so you don't have any stress to pull you away from being an influential leader, and (2) so your people feel free to build rewarding lives for themselves. Those are two reasons, and there are a whole bunch of other drivers for you to create some balance between work and home. What's yours?

The only way to get yourself home in time for dinner is make sure you have a reason to go home. Ah, you knew I'd get to this place, didn't you? By now you've probably figured out this entire book is about who you are becoming as a leader – and as a human being. What's your compelling reason to get a life?

I was talking to one of my clients the other day when Sue said something very profound. She said, "Jen, I'm not sure I have a compelling enough reason to reduce the hours I work. I mean, what would I do with myself if I wasn't working?"

Ah ha! This is a very important point. If you're tried to work less in the past and haven't succeeded, pay attention. The bottom line is you don't have a compelling reason to change. You like your life exactly the way it is. You like being frenzied, burned out, exhausted and tired. Why? Because for most of you, it makes you feel important. It makes you feel as if you're doing something with your life. One of the consultants I work with described this phenomena, "When I look around and see that my desk is a mess, I know I'm doing the right things. I'm making stuff happen, and in a strange way, that unorganized mess makes me feel good."

How on earth do you expect to stop the frenzied pace when it gives you such a tremendous payoff? The answer is, you don't. Every single time you say "I'm working" or "I don't have time," it reinforces how successful you are. You've made the association that if you're busy, you're successful. And if you're not busy, you're a failure.

In my first book, *Work Less, Make More: Stop Working So Hard and Create the Life You Really Want!*, I developed a quiz that may give you some insights you need. Take my Success Rules Quiz and see what shows up.

The Success Rules Quiz

Circle Y for "yes" or N for "no."

1. Do you feel bad if you don't work at least ten hours a day?

    Y   N

2. Do you expect to come home tired from work?

    Y   N

3. Do you act as if your company (the one you own or the one you work for) expects you to put its needs first, your family and your own needs last?

    Y   N

4. Do you feel guilty if you say "no" at work?

    Y   N

5. Do you find yourself taking on more and more work because there's no one else to do it?

    Y   N

6. Is one of your biggest complaints that others don't work as hard as you? Are you secretly proud of this?

    Y   N

7. Do you measure your success by what you achieve through your work, like financial gains and security?

    Y   N

8. Do you keep going and going even when you want to quit?

    Y   N

9. Do you find yourself cutting your vacations short so you can go to the office?

    Y   N

10. Are you frustrated because the results aren't showing up fast enough?

    Y   N

11. Do you typically spend more than ten minutes on a problem without asking for help?

Y   N

12. Are you finding yourself justifying and rationalizing why things are taking so long? You know, excuses like I don't have enough time. It's sitting on someone's desk. I'm waiting for a call back.

Y   N

13. Do you carry your briefcase with you and check your voicemail and emails when you're on vacation?

Y   N

If you said yes to at least three of these, your beliefs about work are limiting your success and ultimately your lifestyle.

You know deep in your body that the frenzied, chaotic pace can only keep up for so long before you start to get sick, divorced or burned out. In fact, I bet many of you are already at that place. You must overcome your belief that success means being busy. To do that, the answer is to create a compelling reason to change. Until the benefit of changing is greater than the payoff you get from being so busy, you will not change.

What's your compelling reason to redesign how you work so you can make it home at a decent hour? Think about your kids, your spouse, the people who are important to you. Do you love them enough to cut back on your work hours? Think about the things you want to accomplish before you leave this place. How much do you truly want to climb Mount Everest or donate your time to a third-world country? I know there are things you're dying to do, you just don't know how to find the time to create a fulfilling life.

What would you do if you had all the time in the world? The answer to that question is your compelling reason to change. Write it down here.

There are probably some of you who are struggling with the answer to this question. I used to work with this wonderful dentist who was challenged by this question. Craig once told me, "Jen, I used to only want to be able to pay my phone bill on time and not have to scrape ice off my windshield in the winter. But now I can afford anything I want. My reason for working so hard has to change."

Craig's compelling reason to work hard and build his company during those difficult years was to make more money, to earn a good living being a dentist. Now years later, Craig has the money he wanted, but his reasons for working didn't change. Instead, he kept working and working without knowing why he was doing it anymore. It became a habit. He was used to working that way, and Craig thought if he stopped working so hard he would lose everything he had built. See how brilliantly our minds play games with us?

As I was coaching Craig, his reason to change was his awakening creative spirit. He wanted to write poetry, get back to songwriting, finish a book he had started. And he was willing to do the work it takes to get there.

Flip back a few pages, and write down your compelling reason to change. The answer could be you want to get a life so your people get a life or it may be more profound than that. I only ask that you give yourself some payoff for changing before going on in this book.

Action step

If you're still struggling with answering this question, here's an exercise that may jar your thoughts. Sit down with a sheet of paper and write out 100 things you want to do before you die. My clients can be so stubborn sometimes that forcing them to come up with 100 accomplishments is often a mind-shattering thing. Most people want to quit when they get to ten or so, but you'll learn a tremendous amount if you push past the natural blocks. Even if it takes you a month, make this list.

One of my clients did this a few weeks back, and we were both surprised to see how much Margie had put aside her adventurous spirit as she was raising her child and taking care of an elderly parent. This list reminded her that travel was an important part of her life, and Margie immediately starting planning some fantastic vacations to take during the next year.

Once your list of 100 is complete, sit back and take a good hard look at what you put on paper. You'll find why you truly want to get a life, and you can use those reasons to make a real difference. Of course you know the next step. Integrate at least one of the things you want during the next day. Lists without action are just that: lists.

MY STORY

This particular topic has a special place in my heart because there was a time when I worked way too much. I was consumed with my work, with achieving and accomplishing, with putting aside anything that would take me off focus from reaching my goals – which by the way were all related to work. Sure, I had an incredible ability to focus in and get what I wanted, but I failed to see how fulfilling life can be when you add in more elements than just work.

My story goes like this. When I started my career, I'm sure I was just like you. I wanted to be massively successful, and to me, that meant climbing the corporate ladder. I grew up in a family where my father worked for a large company for thirty years, and he and my mother told us time and again that working for a big company meant lifelong security. You know, that old "stay there as long as you can so you can retire comfortably" routine. That whole statement just makes me laugh today, but back then working for a large, well-known and prestigious company was the only way to go. The high achiever in me set a goal to be CEO of a billion-dollar company. What the heck, I told myself, it's time for a feisty woman to run the show.

In one of my first jobs, I had the great fortune of working for a very successful man. John was the type of guy who exudes success. At the time, he was driving around in a sweet convertible black Mercedes. He wore Italian suits, had weekly massages in his office and was in the process of building a 4,000 square foot house. So yes, he had the money success brings, but what really got me about John was his charisma. He's the type of guy who would walk into a room, and everyone turns to pay attention to him. He has this aura about him that made you to stop and listen to what he had to say. To top it off, John was young at the time I was working for him. He was probably in his early thirties, and his early success gave me hope that I wouldn't have to wait until I was fifty to make it. Impatience has always been a vice of mine.

One evening I walked into his office, sat down and asked an important question. I said, "John, I want to grow up to be like you. Will you tell me your secret to success?"

You've probably asked someone you admired the same question, and I know you got the same piece of advice. John said, "Jen, you first have to figure out what you want. And then do anything – and I mean anything – to get there." He spent the next hour telling me stories of how much he sacrificed for his career. How many times his friends wanted him to stop working and meet them out for a drink, and how many times he would work until midnight and meet them out only after the work was done. John made it clear that in order to be successful, I needed to give up some things, sacrifice a ton and someday, if I worked hard enough, I'd make it.

This whole story has a familiar ring to it, doesn't it?

It's no surprise that this suffer and sacrifice routine works. It does. I'm always amazed at the human spirit as I watch people put that much effort into their careers. No matter what you put your mind to, you'll probably accomplish it. And that's what I did back then. I stopped working out, meeting with friends, spending time with my family and going to church because I was determined to be successful in my career. That strategy of giving up my life for my job worked – like it has worked for you.

But I paid a pretty high price for that success. Did you?

We all know massively successful people who have failed marriages, bad relationships with their kids, poor health and few true friends. John, the guy I looked up to, was in the midst of his first divorce when I worked with him. (I was so blinded by his success, I didn't see the messed-up relationships.)

Something similar happened to me. I gained thirty pounds, almost got a divorce, ruined my most treasured friendships and lost a sense of who I was. My whole life was defined by what I did for a living. Sure, I was successful at the office, but I was a disaster in life.

How did I wake up? One evening I was eating pizza and drinking beer with my husband when he looked at me from across the table and said, "When are you quitting your job?"

I thought it was a strange question, too. For the next ten minutes, all I did was defend why I could never quit my job. We had a mortgage, car loans, places we wanted to go. I outlined all the financial and material reasons why I had to keep my job. But Steve wouldn't buy my excuses.

He simply looked at me and said, "I don't like who you're becoming."

That comment was my wake-up call. It was a huge slap in the face that I needed. It wasn't pleasant, but boy, was it needed. Once I got through my anger at Steve, I realized he was right. Darn right. I knew I had to find a different way of living so I could be successful and still have an amazing life. That's when I created my Work Less, Make More® philosophy to bring more richness into my own experience without giving up all the benefits success brings.

What about you? Are you going to wait until you get hit on the side of the head before you get a life?

HOW TO GET A LIFE

Up to this point in the book, I've focused a lot of pages to helping you rid yourself of work that doesn't matter and how to focus in on the activities that do. Cleaning off your plate is the first step to getting your life in balance with your work. It's impossible for most people to spend more time at home when their desk is piled high with work to do. I'm assuming you've done the work you needed to do to create some breathing room.

Now let's move on to some other strategies.

1. Set a time to go home. And stick to it.

One of my clients, Greg, had a real issue with this concept. He was complaining one day that his wife was upset with him because he never made it home in order to eat dinner with the family. I couldn't resist asking Greg what the reason was he didn't leave the office on time, and I got a whole bunch of excuses. When we sorted through the excuses, I discovered Greg didn't feel comfortable leaving his office with stuff all over his desk. When he sat down to straighten things up before turning off the lights for the night, he inevitably got caught up in doing something. Most people would tell Greg to get out of his chair at a certain time no matter what. We even tried that for a while, and he set his alarm to leave the office at 6 p.m. This strategy didn't work because he found himself agitated at home because he left his office in such a mess.

Sometimes it's better to admit our idiocracies than try to push past them. So we did the next best thing. Greg gave himself thirty minutes at the end of the day – every day – to go through his piles, check his email and return calls before going home. Before he used to have meetings until 6 p.m., but no longer. When he gave himself the appropriate time to end the day in an ideal way for him, it worked.

I did something similar in my own life. A few years ago, I got a white terrier by the name of Wally. When he was young, I taught Wally to run into my home office every night at 6 p.m. and run around in a circle. This was my signal that it was time to take him for a walk. The second I left the office and got out in the fresh air, I was able to separate my home life with my work life. That's my whole point. Figure out what catalyst need to get yourself out of the office at an appropriate time then do it.

Action step

Set a time that you want to be out of the office. It must be the same time every day as routine is good for the workaholic spirit. Trust me on this one. We're creatures of habit, and you need to build in a new habit of leaving the office at the appropriate time.

Once you decide what time you want to leave every day, your next step is to build in a support system to make sure you hold yourself to your new standard. I've had clients set alarm clocks to remind them it's time to go. Other clients have solicited the help of their co-workers and employees while others pick up the phone and call my voicemail to let me know they're heading out the office. Once the habit is created, they no longer need to call.

The trick is to stand by your new behavior for the next thirty days. That's thirty days in a row because it takes that long for a new habit to take hold. If you're especially stubborn, stay the course for three months.

2. Take more vacations.

I bet some of you laughed when you read this because you're thinking to yourself, "Great idea, Jen, but who's going to do the work while I'm gone?" That's how I would have reacted five years ago when I hadn't taken a vacation in three years!

Think back to the last time you went on vacation. What happened during the week before you left for your time off? Yes, you got it. You got more work done during those five days than the entire month before. That's always what happens before you leave on a trip. You have this immediate push and urgency to get things off the plate and completed. You go through your email and trash things that don't matter. You throw piles of paper away that you know you don't need. You call all the people you wanted to call but were procrastinating about. And that's simply the little things. I've seen my clients close huge deals right before they left because they had urgency to get the job done. Take more vacations and watch your productivity soar.

Action step

If you don't already have a good travel agent, walk around the office and ask your co-workers and colleagues whom they recommend. Then pick up the phone or send an email with your vacation schedule for the next two years and ask the agent to schedule out your trips. You can arrange to have him or her create an entire two-year vacation schedule with the appropriate deposits spread out over the year. If you can afford it, it's best to pay all the deposits up front so you'll prevent yourself from cancelling the trips when you're financially committed. It's rare I've seen someone cancel their trip when they've already paid for it.

Please do not fall back into the do-it-yourself mode. That's one of the reasons you don't take more vacations because you're forcing yourself to do the research which takes time. Delegate this one off to someone who specializes in this. Give them a budget and schedule your vacations. Right now.

3. Work from home one day a week.

There's nothing like spending the day in your pajamas to refresh your spirit. As I've mentioned before, distraction is the real enemy today. You have to eliminate what takes you off course and give yourself the opportunity to get some work done. And maybe even take a nap in the afternoon.

The leaders I work with who spend one day at home every week are much more productive. They don't have to spend time commuting, and they use that extra time to crank through some projects. It's a lot easier to get a life when you build in some breathing room. You won't feel guilty, and you'll be able to have it all.

Action step

Open your calendar right now and block out one day in the next two weeks where you can work from home. Then give it a try. If it gives you the feeling that your personal productivity soars, build it into your regular schedule. If you find yourself distracted by dirty laundry or household chores, maybe grabbing a laptop and going to the library will give you the quiet time you need. My point: do something this week to get yourself out of the office and build space in your life to get the most important work done.

GIVING YOUR PEOPLE TIME FOR A LIFE

It's easy for you to sit back and think that helping your people get a life isn't your job. Isn't that their responsibility? There's something to be said about this line of thinking. If you have a bunch of workaholic employees, nothing will change until they decide they want to change. I'll give you that.

Yet at the same time, it's vital that you set up the environment – and your supporting behavior – to give them that choice. Many employees don't feel as if it's okay with the boss to take more time off, and we need to eliminate that excuse right now.

Here are six strategies that have worked with other leaders. They may help you help your people get a life.

1. **Never disturb them when they're on vacation or home sick. Never.**

When I'm at booksignings or speaking in front of large audiences, folks always come up to me after my presentation and tell me some horror story about the person they work for. These horror stories more times than not have to do with managers who insist on calling their people while they're away on some luxurious vacation in Mexico. This behavior is very common – and very annoying.

Are your systems so poor that you can't allow your staff to take seven days off? Stop calling them when they're not in the office. Build solid back-up systems so you don't rely on one person as much as you do. Give your people a well-deserved break without having to worry about. They need it – and so do you.

2. Walk around the office right before you leave and make sure they're packing up to go.

Yes, that means you can be a support for your people who are always trying to break their obsession with being at the office. If you truly understand how important it is for your team to get a life, you would gladly walk around the office every evening to make sure they were going home. Every one of us needs a kick in the butt from time to time, and this may be exactly what your team needs. It's one thing to say you're going home at a decent hour, it's quite another actually do it. Be the catalyst your team needs.

3. Make sure your people take their allotted vacation time.

This seems easy enough, but when project after project is coming down the pike, it's hard as heck to remember to take your own vacations let alone anyone else's. One of my clients Anne solved this problem for herself and her team. She invited a travel agent to their weekly staff meetings every week for an entire month. The travel agent would share two different destinations to travel to each week, and she brought short videos to watch and brochures to flip through. Anne's assistant would arrange to have food that reflected those vacation spots at the meeting. One week it was a Mexican fiesta, the next week a Hawaiian luau. Anne even asked a local day spa representative to come to her staff meetings for those employees who wanted an easier get-away than having to jump on a plane. The staff could sign up for ten-minute chair massages on that day.

Anne took this vacation stuff seriously. She started using trips as performance incentives which helped employees who couldn't afford to drop $3,000 on an exotic vacation. So far the people who have earned the trips were the ones who hadn't been on a real vacation in years. You should see how refreshed those folks were when they came back after a week on the beach.

4. Give them the chance to work from home once a week. Or more.

Your productivity goes through the roof when you have quiet time, your team probably needs the same thing. With today's work environments full of cubicles, it's easy to get pushed off course in the midst of a crazy day. That doesn't happen when you're at home with only the dog to distract you.

Too many leaders frown on their employees' desire to work at home. The fundamental reason which few will admit is they don't trust their people. There's this underlying belief that if you're not in the office, you must be goofing off. Grow up, will you? Today's leaders do not have the time or energy to sit on their people. You have got to break this belief that being in the office is the only way to prove you're doing the work.

For those employees who have kids at home, be sure to provide laptop computers so anyone can go to the local coffee shop or bookstore to get some quiet time. If you want your people to do their best work, create the environment that allows them to do that. And sometimes the best environment is not at your office.

5. Let people work when they want to work.

One morning, one of my assistants Kim called my office to let me know she was leaving in order to go to the drugstore. She started the conversation by saying, "I know you don't care about this, but I'm going to Osco." To which I said, "You're right. I don't care. Why are you calling me?" Kim had just started working with us, and she was testing the waters to see if what I said was really true. Was it possible for her to work for someone who fully trusts she'll get the job done? She got her answer, and now I don't get calls from her telling me where she's going every minute of the day.

We have a rule at my company: results matter. What doesn't matter is how or when someone gets the job done. That does-n't mean we work slowly or we don't have strict deadlines. We do. It means that some people on my team like to write email at 7 a.m. while others are in the office until 7 p.m. because they showed up at 9 a.m. Other times people will work all weekend then take a few days off during the week. It's the flexibility they adore and appreciate.

This is an especially hard for many leaders who like to know where their people are. Again, it's a matter of trust. If you don't trust your people, you'll wonder if they're doing their jobs when you don't see them. Leadership today is based on trust. You hire the right people then let them do their jobs however they want to do it. If they aren't performing, address that, but don't think putting your thumb down and forcing someone to work when you want them to work is the answer. Flexibility matters in today's fast-paced world.

Yes, I fully admit these flexible work hours won't work for every position. Someone needs to be there answering the phones, and the assembly lines need to be working so many hours a day. Many of your professional jobs, however, don't demand stringent work hours. Trust your people, and build flexibility in their work day.

6. Follow the strategies in this book and make sure they know what matters.

It takes an incredibly strong person to be able to leave the office when there's so much left to do. My husband has this saying, "The work will be there tomorrow." He has the capacity to leave his office and leave work behind. I don't. My strategy has been to design my business to ensure that we don't get caught up in the too much to do syndrome. My intention is to walk away every night without feeling guilty because everything is handled in some way. Or it's on the schedule to be completed in the very near future.

That's what I want for you. Integrate the strategies I've outlined in this book, and I guarantee you'll have the space you need to get a life. Your people will be able to do their jobs in less time because they won't be distracted by your annoying habits. And they'll know what activities matter and what they can let go.

Action step

If you're interested in doing more work on this Get A Life process, please pick up a copy of my first book, *Work Less, Make More: Stop Working So Hard and Create the Life You Really Want!* It's full of more than 100 exercises that will help you break your obsession with work. People have told me it's the wake-up call they need to dramatically change how they work and live, and it may be what you need if this is a real problem area for you.

YOUR LIFE: ARE YOU LIVING THE LIFE YOU WANT TO LIVE?

The reason I ask that question is often I find leaders are so caught up in being the boss, the person in charge, that they fail to ask themselves this important question. Is your life the way you want it to be?

At the end of the day, I want you to look back on the time you invested and say, "Yes! I did exactly what I wanted to do." There are some of you who want to work at the intensity that you do. Others who want to spend more time with the people you love. Many of you want to have both: an amazing career and a richly satisfying life.

Unless you constantly ask yourself if you're living the way you want to live, you're going to wake up one day and wonder what happened to your life. Too many people I know are sleep walking. They don't even ask themselves what life they want to live because they're too busy checking things off their To-Do lists, putting out fires and handling employee issues. Then one day they wake up and wonder what happened. Regrets and guilt kick in because they know deep in their hearts that they spent time at the office that they wanted to invest somewhere else. But they were too unconscious to change their focus or too weak to push back on the things they didn't want to do.

Accomplishments and achievements are one thing. Relationships, now those are the things that define your life. It's the people who bring your joy, satisfaction and a smile on your life. Yet the sad truth is it's the relationships in your life that suffer when you're on the fast track, when you're in hyperdrive to accomplish even more. It's easy to think that someday you'll spend time with the people you love, but that someday never comes, does it?

Be one of the strong ones, the ones who live their lives exactly as they want to live them. As a leader, you have a great capacity to create whatever you want at the office. Are you using that skill to build a fulfilling life?

If you don't, who will? It's your life after all. Not theirs.

So I ask again: Are you living the life you want to live? If the answer is no, then by all means, make the necessary changes. Focus on driving yourself wild. Everything – your success at work and in life – depends on it.

IT DRIVES THEM CRAZY WHEN . . .

1. You work 80-hour work weeks, but you say it's okay for them to go home. They don't believe you.
2. You call them on nights and weekends.
3. You send email in the middle of the night.
4. You don't give them time off after they've worked a particularly intense period of time.
5. You call them when they're on vacation. Or expect them to check voicemail and email while they're away.
6. You show up stressed out, rude and edgy. And you won't go on vacation.
7. You believe that they have to suffer and sacrifice for success.
8. You're amazed when no one wants to follow in your shoes. Why would they want a life like yours?
9. You believe success at work means success at life.
10. You don't have a life. They feel incredibly sad for you.

IT DRIVES THEM WILD WHEN . . .

1. You love your life as much as you love your work. They strive to follow in your footsteps.
2. You trust them enough to work from home now and again.
3. You make sure they take all their allotted vacation time.
4. You don't call them during the evening or on the weekends. Except in extreme circumstances.
5. You get mad at them when they call in while on vacation. You tell them to sit on the beach and relax. Then you hang up the phone.

6.   You allow them to work flexible schedules so they can integrate their family responsibilities with their work.

7.   You understand that life success is different than work success.

8.   You give them free rein to work however they want as long as they get the right results.

9.   You show up the majority of the time in a good mood.

10.   You have an amazing life as well as an amazing career. And it feels good.

Final notes

It's funny, but when I was in the throes of writing this book, I started having second thoughts about being a leader. I was going through a particularly difficult time dealing with hypergrowth in my business, and the demands on my time and energy were becoming extreme. I yearned to be a Lone Ranger again, to go back to my simple Work Less, Make More® lifestyle. I'm sure it's no coincidence that I went through this crisis while I was writing.

'VE SAID IT BEFORE, and I'll say it again: being a leader is tough. I think it's even more difficult than being married. At least in marriage you only have one person to deal with. In today's fast-moving economy, most leaders have a herd of cats to manage, and we have days where we want to give up.

But here I am, on the last few pages of this book, and I've decided being a leader is worth it. When push comes to shove, I've never done anything more exhilarating than this. I love watching my coaching team reach new heights with the direction I give them. I'm inspired by seeing my vision unfold in exciting new areas, and I'm constantly challenged by doing things differently. And better. I discovered through writing this book that if you're a leader in your heart, you *have to be* a leader. It's your calling, your mission, your reason for being. And as a leader, you are the one who can make a huge impact on the world.

It's true that our work environments are crazed and chaotic. I also know this seven-step coaching process I've developed takes a lot of work to implement. It's tough to change your leadership style. It's tough to lead maverick, feisty employees who are threatening to leave. And it's difficult to deal with the changes and problems hitting your desk every day.

Here's what I also know: if anyone can influence the workplace, it's you. You're the one who can stand in the middle of the fire and do what's right. You're the one who can help your people focus on what truly matters then push them out the door when it's time to go home. You're the one who can give them the opportunity they need to inspire their souls. And you're the one who can bring the love back into the game of business.

If you don't, who will? I want this *Drive Your People Wild Without Driving Them Crazy* philosophy to be your wake-up call. I imagine a world where our people are performing at high levels in companies they adore while still making it home in time for dinner. But only if you have the strength and courage to make this real.

I've seen my clients produce amazing results with this coaching work, and I know you're just like them. You want to be the best of the best. You want to inspire your team. You want to become the powerful leader you know you can be.

All we need now is some action. It's one thing to say you want to inspire your people, it's quite another to actually do it. The rest of this journey is up to you, my friend. Are you going to drive them crazy or are you going to drive them wild?

You know the right answer. Now go out and make it happen.

About the author

Jennifer White, MCC is one of the world's most sought-after executive coaches. She is founder and CEO of The JWC Group, Inc., an executive coaching firm known for its innovative products and services. Their clients include Fidelity Investments, Procter & Gamble and hundreds of small businesses. The coaching team guides leaders to create thriving businesses and richly satisfying lives.

Jennifer is the author of the best-selling book, *Work Less, Make More: Stop Working So Hard and Create the Life You Really Want!*, now in its third printing. A nationally syndicated columnist, she is recognized as a leading authority on success, and Jennifer speaks to a wide variety of audiences on many of the topics you read in this book. She's appeared in hundreds of publications including *USA Today*, the *Washington Post*, *Entrepreneur Magazine* and *Black Enterprise Magazine*. Jennifer also serves on the board of directors with the International Coach Federation.

She lives in Kansas City with her husband and their seven pets.

You can reach the author at **help@wildorcrazy.com**.

About The JWC Group, Inc.

One thing we know about *Drive Your People Wild Without Driving Them Crazy*™ is that it's more than just a book. It's a new way of leading in the business world.

Change is hard, and it can be difficult. Sometimes you can't do it alone. Many people like to read all the books that tell them how to become more successful, but somehow they just don't apply what they're learning. Don't let that happen to you.

We've developed a variety of specific programs to help you integrate these concepts into your organization. We have developed a powerful corporate coaching program you can bring into your organization, and we train an exclusive group of internal and external coaches on our methodology. To learn more, visit us at: **www.wildorcrazy.com**

We also conduct in-house training programs, keynote speeches and executive coaching/consulting services. Call us. We want to hear from you.

The JWC Group, Inc.
(877) 967-6637
help@wildorcrazy.com
www.wildorcrazy.com

Index